2003-2004 Supplement
National Security Law

Third Edition

Stephen Dycus
Professor of Law
Vermont Law School

Arthur L. Berney
Professor of Law, Emeritus
Boston College

William C. Banks
Laura J. and L. Douglas Meredith Professor
Syracuse University

Peter Raven-Hansen
Glen Earl Weston Research Professor of Law
George Washington University

1185 Avenue of the Americas, New York, NY 10036
www.aspenpublishers.com

© 2003 Stephen Dycus, Arthur L. Berney, William C. Banks, and Peter Raven-Hansen

All rights reserved. No part of this publication may be reproduced or transmitted in any form or by any means, electronic or mechanical, including photocopy, recording, or any information storage and retrieval system, without permission in writing from the publisher. Requests for permission to make copies of any part of this publication should be mailed to:

> Permissions
> Aspen Publishers
> 1185 Avenue of the Americas
> New York, NY 10036

Printed in the United States of America

1 2 3 4 5 6 7 8 9 0

ISBN 0 - 7355 - 4500 - 6

Library of Congress Cataloging-in-Publication Data

National security law / Stephen Dycus . . . [et al.] – 3rd ed.
    p. cm.
  Includes index.
  ISBN 0-7355-2823-3 (casebook)
  ISBN 0-7355-4500-6 (supplement)
  1. National security – Law and legislation – United States.
    I. Dycus, Stephen.

KF4651.N377 2002
343.73'01 – dc21   2001058379

About Aspen Publishers

Aspen Publishers, headquartered in New York City, is a leading information provider for attorneys, business professionals, and law students. Written by preeminent authorities, our products consist of analytical and practical information covering both U.S. and international topics. We publish in the full range of formats, including updated manuals, books, periodicals, CDs, and online products.

Our proprietary content is complemented by 2,500 legal databases, containing over 11 million documents, available through our Loislaw division. Aspen Publishers also offers a wide range of topical legal and business databases linked to Loislaw's primary material. Our mission is to provide accurate, timely, and authoritative content in easily accessible formats, supported by unmatched customer care.

To order any Aspen Publishers title, go to *www.aspenpublishers.com* or call 1-800-638-8437.

To reinstate your manual update service, call 1-800-638-8437.

For more information on Loislaw products, go to *www.loislaw.com* or call 1-800-364-2512.

For Customer Care issues, e-mail *CustomerCare@aspenpublishers.com*; call 1-800-234-1660; or fax 1-800-901-9075.

Aspen Publishers
A Wolters Kluwer Company

EDITORIAL ADVISORS

Erwin Chemerinsky
Sydney M. Irmas Professor of Public Interest Law, Legal Ethics, and Political Science
University of Southern California

Richard A. Epstein
James Parker Hall Distinguished Service Professor of Law
University of Chicago

Ronald J. Gilson
Charles J. Meyers Professor of Law and Business
Stanford University
Marc and Eva Stern Professor of Law and Business
Columbia University

James E. Krier
Earl Warren DeLano Professor of Law
University of Michigan

Richard K. Neumann, Jr.
Professor of Law
Hofstra University School of Law

Kent D. Syverud
Dean and Garner Anthony Professor
Vanderbilt University Law School

Elizabeth Warren
Leo Gottlieb Professor of Law
Harvard University

EMERITUS EDITORIAL ADVISORS

E. Allan Farnsworth
Alfred McCormack Professor of Law
Columbia University

Geoffrey C. Hazard, Jr.
Trustee Professor of Law
University of Pennsylvania

Bernard Wolfman
Fessenden Professor of Law
Harvard University

Contents

Preface ix
Table of Cases xi

Chapter 4. The President's National Security Powers   *1*

A. Foreign Relations Powers   1

Chapter 8. General War   *3*

E. War Against Iraq – 2003   3
         Authorization for Use of Military Force Against
           Iraq Resolution of 2002   3
         Notes and Questions   8

Chapter 10. Intelligence Operations   *11*

C. Problems in the Reform of Intelligence Operations   11
    2. Executive Branch Reforms   11
F. The Privatization of Intelligence Operations   11
    2. Dirty Assets   11

Contents

Chapter 11. Organizing for Counterterrorism: An Overview   *13*

A. Countering Terrorism at Home and Abroad   13
    1. Defining the Terrorist Threat   13
       a. What Is Terrorism?   13
          People's Mojahedin Organization of Iran v. Department of State   13
          Notes and Questions   17
    2. Planning for Homeland Security   18

Chapter 12. Investigating Terrorism and Other National Security Threats   *19*

B. The Fourth Amendment Framework   19
    4. Investigations Abroad   19
C. Congressional Authority for Surveillance: The Foreign Intelligence Surveillance Act   20
       In re: Sealed Case No. 02-001, 02-002   24
       Notes and Questions   38
D. Executive Authority for National Security Investigations   40
    1. Initiating Investigation   40
    2. Choosing and Regulating the Means of Investigation   44
E. Profiling Suspects for Investigations   46
F. Preventive Detention   47
       Office of the Inspector General, Department of Justice, Press Release, The September 11 Detainees   47

Chapter 13. Consequence Management: When the Worst Happens   *55*

B. Who's in Charge? Taking Command of the Situation   55
    2. Addressing Medical Emergencies   55

	c. Civil Liberties Implications	55
C.	Special Threats to Civil Liberties in a Crisis	56
	1.1. Military Detention	56
	Ex parte Milligan	57
	Ex parte Quirin	57
	Hamdi v. Rumsfeld	57
	Padilla v. Bush	69
	Notes and Questions	84

Chapter 14. Trying International Terrorists — 91

A.	Criminalizing Sedition, Terrorism, and Support for Terrorism	91
D.	Trying Terrorists and Other International Criminals	92
	1. Secret Information in Proceedings Against Terrorists	92
	Note on United States v. Moussaoui	92
	Notes and Questions	94

Chapter 15. Public Access to National Security Information — 99

A.	Executive Order No. 12,958 – Classified National Security Information	99
B.	The Freedom of Information Act	100
	1. The Statutory Text	100
	2. Statutory Exemptions and Judicial Review	100
	Center for National Security Studies v. United States Department of Justice	101
	Notes and Questions	114
D.	Common Law Right to Know	116
E.	Constitutional Right to Know	117
	Detroit Free Press v. Ashcroft	118
	North Jersey Media Group, Inc. v. Ashcroft	134
	Notes and Questions	145
F.	Protecting "State Secrets" in Civil Litigation	147

Preface

Publication of this Supplement for a casebook that has been in print for only a year is proof – if any were needed – of the dynamic character of National Security Law. Hardly a week goes by without some new judicial decision or executive act that changes our understanding of how government works to protect us and protect the values we hold dear. Keeping abreast of these changes presents a challenge for students, teachers, and practitioners alike. It also presents wonderful new opportunities for learning about the legal process.

The materials in this Supplement reflect the nation's continuing anxiety in the wake of the September 11, 2001, terrorist attacks. They illustrate in new ways the sharp tensions between security and liberty that arise during any great national crisis. They restate important questions about the separation of powers among the three branches of government. And they call on us to consider the extent to which emergency measures – and their attendant sacrifices – will now become the norm.

In the current climate of fear, the executive branch has predictably become the "first responder" at the federal level, using military and executive orders to push the envelope of existing legal authority. Congress has followed at a short distance, appearing to take the executive at its word in enacting defense-related legislation. The courts have followed reluctantly at a greater distance, waiting until cases come to them, but sometimes prolonging the wait by declining on various grounds to become involved.

Yet there is evidence that this pattern may already have begun to shift. The executive branch is providing more information about some of its responses, as well as some tentative self-criticism. The Justice Department Inspector General's recent report on the detention of aliens on immigration charges is an example. Members of both parties in Congress have mounted inquiries into the Bush administration's justifications for the 2003 war in Iraq. And a number of federal courts have recently ruled against the government in cases implicating the national security, rebuffing efforts, for example, to deny an "enemy combatant" access to counsel, to close depor-

Preface

tation hearings, and to restrain publication of a book about Chinese nuclear weapons.

Clearly, the materials presented here are not the last word. More than ever before, the reader must keep abreast of the news and must relate each day's developments to the legal and political framework set forth in the casebook and this Supplement. Most important, we must look for ways to use our training and experience to help shape these developments in the future.

Two organizational issues deserve mention here. What we called "preventive detention" in Chapter 12 of the casebook has given way in several significant recent cases to military detention. Although we talked about such detention in Chapter 13, the authority for it is said to rest on the military commission cases discussed in Chapter 14. In this Supplement, we suggest reading these casebook materials out of the original order, together with new cases and discussion included here, to create a more nearly coherent unit on military detention.

"Consequence management" was already an unruly subject when we wrote the casebook, and "Homeland Security" was simply jargon, not a department. At this writing it is not clear that the newly created department has yet become much more than jargon. Beyond noting its creation, therefore, we were hard-pressed here to identify materials that would give it much content. Further analysis will come later.

We are grateful to our adopters and to many friends in the national security community who have kept us informed of developments and made suggestions for continuing improvements in the casebook. We also wish to thank our research assistants, Steven Zimmerman at George Washington University Law School and Sara Baynard, Edward Demetriou, Abigail Doolittle, Robin Longe, and Emily Wetherell at Vermont Law School, as well as our copyeditor, Barbara Rappaport, for their help in preparing this Supplement. Finally, we are grateful to Kathy Yoon, Peggy Rehberger, and Carol McGeehan of Aspen Publishers for their encouragement and support.

Stephen Dycus
William C. Banks
Peter Raven-Hansen

July 2003

Table of Cases

Al-Marri, United States v., 87
American Civil Liberties Union v. United States, 38
American Civil Liberties Union v. United States Department of Justice, 23
American Insurance Assn. v. Garamendi, 1
Application of the United States for a Material Witness Warrant, In re, 52
Awadallah, United States v., 52

Burr, United States v., 52
Burrows v. Superior Court, 23

Center for National Security Studies v. United States Department of Justice, 53, **101**, 116, 117, 145
Chavez v. Martinez, 19
Christopher v. Harbury, 12
Coalition of Clergy v. Bush, 88

Dames & Moore v. Regan, 2
Denmore v. Hyung Joon Kim, 51, 53
Detroit Free Press v. Ashcroft, 118
Doe v. Tenet, 148

Ex parte _____. *See* name of party.

Hamdi v. Rumsfeld, 57
Harbury v. Deutch, 89
Herring, In re, 147

In re _____. *See* name of party.

Johnson v. Eisentrager, 89, 94

McDonnell Douglas Corp. v. United States, 148
Miller, United States v., 21, 23
Milligan, Ex parte, 56, **57**, 86
Moussaoui, United States v., 92, 93, 94, 95, 146, 147

North Jersey Media Group, Inc. v. Ashcroft, 134

Table of Cases

Odah v. United States, 86, 88

Padilla v. Bush, 69
People's Mojahedin Organization of Iran v. Department of State, 13
Prize Cases, 85

Quirin, Ex parte, 56, **57**, 84, 86

Reynolds, United States v., 147

Salerno, United States v., 51
Sealed Case No. 02-001, 02-002, In re, 24
Smith v. Maryland, 20, 21

Trulock v. Lee, 148

United States v. _____. *See* name of party.

Verdugo-Urquidez, United States v., 89

4

The President's National Security Powers

A. FOREIGN RELATIONS POWERS

Page 70. Add this material after Note 8.

9. *What Counts as Foreign Policy?* In American Insurance Assn. v. Garamendi, 123 S. Ct. 2374 (2003), the Supreme Court struck down a California statute requiring insurance companies to disclose information about insurance policies that they or related companies sold to Europeans during the Holocaust era. There was no federal statute on point. Executive agreements between the United States and Germany, Austria, and France encouraged a voluntary International Commission on Holocaust Era Insurance Claims (ICHEIC) to become the exclusive forum for claims on such policies, but they did not expressly forbid other remedies for claimants. Federal preemption was found on the basis of "interference with the foreign policy those agreements embody." 123 S. Ct. at 2387.

Justice Souter noted for the 5-4 majority that, because of the need for uniformity, state power is preempted by national government policy in the field of foreign relations.

> Nor is there any question generally that there is executive authority to decide what that policy should be. Although the source of the President's power to act in foreign affairs does not enjoy any textual detail, the historical gloss on the "executive Power" vested in Article II of the Constitution has recognized the President's "vast share of responsibility for the conduct of our foreign relations." Youngstown Sheet & Tube Co. v. Sawyer, 343 U.S. 579, 610-611 (1952) (Frankfurter, J., concurring). While Congress holds express authority to regulate public and private dealings with other nations in its war and foreign commerce powers, in

foreign affairs the President has a degree of independent authority to act.

At a more specific level, our cases have recognized that the President has authority to make "executive agreements" with other countries, requiring no ratification by the Senate or approval by Congress, this power having been exercised since the early years of the Republic. . . . Given the fact that the practice goes back over 200 years to the first Presidential administration, and has received congressional acquiescence throughout its history, the conclusion "[t]hat the President's control of foreign relations includes the settlement of claims is indisputable."

Generally, then, valid executive agreements are fit to preempt state law, just as treaties are, and if the agreements here had expressly preempted laws like [the California statute], the issue would be straightforward. But petitioners and the United States as *amicus curiae* both have to acknowledge that the agreements include no preemption clause, and so leave their claim of preemption to rest on asserted interference with the foreign policy those agreements embody. . . .

. . . [However,] the likelihood that state legislation will produce something more than incidental effect in conflict with express foreign policy of the National Government would require preemption of the state law. And . . . it would be reasonable to consider the strength of the state interest, judged by standards of traditional practice, when deciding how serious a conflict must be shown before declaring the state law preempted. Judged by these standards, we think petitioners and the Government have demonstrated a sufficiently clear conflict to require finding preemption here. . . .

. . . [I]t is worth noting that Congress has done nothing to express disapproval of the President's policy. Legislation along the lines of [the California law] has been introduced in Congress repeatedly, but none of the bills has come close to making it into law. In sum, Congress has not acted on the matter addressed here. Given the President's independent authority "in the areas of foreign policy and national security, . . . congressional silence is not to be equated with congressional disapproval." Haig v. Agee, 453 U.S. 280, 291 (1981). [123 S. Ct. at 2384.]

The dissenters complained that no executive agreement mentioned the state's sole concern: public disclosure. *Id.* at 2399 (Ginsberg, J., dissenting). They also noted that in cases like Dames & Moore v. Regan, 453 U.S. 654 (1981) (casebook p. 115), the Court gave effect to the express terms of an executive agreement. 123 S. Ct. at 2401. Do you think the Court should require a clearer statement of conflicting foreign policy before finding preemption? By relying on inference and implication, has the Court itself effectively become an expositor of foreign policy?

8

General War

Page 333. Add these materials at end of chapter.

E. WAR AGAINST IRAQ – 2003

Authorization for Use of Military Force Against Iraq Resolution of 2002
Pub. L. No. 107-243, 116 Stat. 1498
October 16, 2002

Whereas in 1990 in response to Iraq's war of aggression against and illegal occupation of Kuwait, the United States forged a coalition of nations to liberate Kuwait and its people in order to defend the national security of the United States and enforce United Nations Security Council resolutions relating to Iraq;

Whereas after the liberation of Kuwait in 1991, Iraq entered into a United Nations sponsored cease-fire agreement pursuant to which Iraq unequivocally agreed, among other things, to eliminate its nuclear, biological, and chemical weapons programs and the means to deliver and develop them, and to end its support for international terrorism;

Whereas the efforts of international weapons inspectors, United States intelligence agencies, and Iraqi defectors led to the discovery that Iraq had large stockpiles of chemical weapons and a large scale biological weapons program, and that Iraq had an advanced nuclear weapons development program that was much closer to producing a nuclear weapon than intelligence reporting had previously indicated;

Whereas Iraq, in direct and flagrant violation of the cease-fire, attempted to thwart the efforts of weapons inspectors to identify and destroy Iraq's weapons of mass destruction stockpiles and development capabilities, which finally resulted in the withdrawal of inspectors from Iraq on October 31, 1998;

Whereas in Public Law 105-235 (August 14, 1998), Congress concluded that Iraq's continuing weapons of mass destruction programs threatened vital United States interests and international peace and security, declared Iraq to be in "material and unacceptable breach of its international obligations" and urged the President "to take appropriate action, in accordance with the Constitution and relevant laws of the United States, to bring Iraq into compliance with its international obligations";

Whereas Iraq both poses a continuing threat to the national security of the United States and international peace and security in the Persian Gulf region and remains in material and unacceptable breach of its international obligations by, among other things, continuing to possess and develop a significant chemical and biological weapons capability, actively seeking a nuclear weapons capability, and supporting and harboring terrorist organizations;

Whereas Iraq persists in violating resolution[s] of the United Nations Security Council by continuing to engage in brutal repression of its civilian population thereby threatening international peace and security in the region, by refusing to release, repatriate, or account for non-Iraqi citizens wrongfully detained by Iraq, including an American serviceman, and by failing to return property wrongfully seized by Iraq from Kuwait;

Whereas the current Iraqi regime has demonstrated its capability and willingness to use weapons of mass destruction against other nations and its own people;

Whereas the current Iraqi regime has demonstrated its continuing hostility toward, and willingness to attack, the United States, including by attempting in 1993 to assassinate former President Bush and by firing on many thousands of occasions on United States and Coalition Armed Forces engaged in enforcing the resolutions of the United Nations Security Council;

Whereas members of al Qaida, an organization bearing responsibility for attacks on the United States, its citizens, and interests, including the attacks that occurred on September 11, 2001, are known to be in Iraq;

Whereas Iraq continues to aid and harbor other international terrorist organizations, including organizations that threaten the lives and safety of United States citizens;

Whereas the attacks on the United States of September 11, 2001, underscored the gravity of the threat posed by the acquisition of weapons of mass destruction by international terrorist organizations;

Whereas Iraq's demonstrated capability and willingness to use weapons of mass destruction, the risk that the current Iraqi regime will either employ those weapons to launch a surprise attack against the United States or its

Chapter 8. General War

Armed Forces or provide them to international terrorists who would do so, and the extreme magnitude of harm that would result to the United States and its citizens from such an attack, combine to justify action by the United States to defend itself;

Whereas United Nations Security Council Resolution 678 (1990) authorizes the use of all necessary means to enforce United Nations Security Council Resolution 660 (1990) and subsequent relevant resolutions and to compel Iraq to cease certain activities that threaten international peace and security, including the development of weapons of mass destruction and refusal or obstruction of United Nations weapons inspections in violation of United Nations Security Council Resolution 687 (1991), repression of its civilian population in violation of United Nations Security Council Resolution 688 (1991), and threatening its neighbors or United Nations operations in Iraq in violation of United Nations Security Council Resolution 949 (1994);

Whereas in the Authorization for Use of Military Force Against Iraq Resolution (Public Law 102-1), Congress has authorized the President "to use United States Armed Forces pursuant to United Nations Security Council Resolution 678 (1990) in order to achieve implementation of Security Council Resolutions 660, 661, 662, 664, 665, 666, 667, 669, 670, 674, and 677";

Whereas in December 1991, Congress expressed its sense that it "supports the use of all necessary means to achieve the goals of United Nations Security Council Resolution 687 as being consistent with the Authorization of Use of Military Force Against Iraq Resolution (Public Law 102-1)," that Iraq's repression of its civilian population violates United Nations Security Council Resolution 688 and "constitutes a continuing threat to the peace, security, and stability of the Persian Gulf region," and that Congress "supports the use of all necessary means to achieve the goals of United Nations Security Council Resolution 688";

Whereas the Iraq Liberation Act of 1998 (Public Law 105-338) expressed the sense of Congress that it should be the policy of the United States to support efforts to remove from power the current Iraqi regime and promote the emergence of a democratic government to replace that regime;

Whereas on September 12, 2002, President Bush committed the United States to "work with the United Nations Security Council to meet our common challenge" posed by Iraq and to "work for the necessary resolutions," while also making clear that "the Security Council resolutions will be enforced, and the just demands of peace and security will be met, or action will be unavoidable";

Whereas the United States is determined to prosecute the war on terrorism and Iraq's ongoing support for international terrorist groups combined with its development of weapons of mass destruction in direct violation of its obligations under the 1991 cease-fire and other United Nations Security Council resolutions make clear that it is in the national security interests of the United States and in furtherance of the war on terrorism that all relevant United Nations Security Council resolutions be enforced, including through the use of force if necessary;

Whereas Congress has taken steps to pursue vigorously the war on terrorism through the provision of authorities and funding requested by the President to take the necessary actions against international terrorists and terrorist organizations, including those nations, organizations, or persons who planned, authorized, committed, or aided the terrorist attacks that occurred on September 11, 2001, or harbored such persons or organizations;

Whereas the President and Congress are determined to continue to take all appropriate actions against international terrorists and terrorist organizations, including those nations, organizations, or persons who planned, authorized, committed, or aided the terrorist attacks that occurred on September 11, 2001, or harbored such persons or organizations;

Whereas the President has authority under the Constitution to take action in order to deter and prevent acts of international terrorism against the United States, as Congress recognized in the joint resolution on Authorization for Use of Military Force (Public Law 107-40); and

Whereas it is in the national security interests of the United States to restore international peace and security to the Persian Gulf region: Now, therefore, be it

Resolved by the Senate and House of Representatives of the United States of America in Congress assembled . . .

Sec. 2. Support for United States Diplomatic Efforts

The Congress of the United States supports the efforts by the President to –

(1) strictly enforce through the United Nations Security Council all relevant Security Council resolutions regarding Iraq and encourages him in those efforts; and

(2) obtain prompt and decisive action by the Security Council to ensure that Iraq abandons its strategy of delay, evasion and noncompliance and promptly and strictly complies with all relevant Security Council resolutions regarding Iraq.

Sec. 3. Authorization for Use of United States Armed Forces

(a) AUTHORIZATION – The President is authorized to use the Armed Forces of the United States as he determines to be necessary and appropriate in order to –

(1) defend the national security of the United States against the continuing threat posed by Iraq; and
(2) enforce all relevant United Nations Security Council resolutions regarding Iraq.

(b) PRESIDENTIAL DETERMINATION – In connection with the exercise of the authority granted in subsection (a) to use force the President shall, prior to such exercise or as soon thereafter as may be feasible, but no later than 48 hours after exercising such authority, make available to the Speaker of the House of Representatives and the President pro tempore of the Senate his determination that –

(1) reliance by the United States on further diplomatic or other peaceful means alone either (A) will not adequately protect the national security of the United States against the continuing threat posed by Iraq or (B) is not likely to lead to enforcement of all relevant United Nations Security Council resolutions regarding Iraq; and
(2) acting pursuant to this joint resolution is consistent with the United States and other countries continuing to take the necessary actions against international terrorist and terrorist organizations, including those nations, organizations, or persons who planned, authorized, committed or aided the terrorist attacks that occurred on September 11, 2001.

(c) WAR POWERS RESOLUTION REQUIREMENTS –

(1) SPECIFIC STATUTORY AUTHORIZATION – Consistent with section 8(a)(1) of the War Powers Resolution, the Congress declares that this section is intended to constitute specific statutory authorization within the meaning of section 5(b) of the War Powers Resolution.
(2) APPLICABILITY OF OTHER REQUIREMENTS – Nothing in this joint resolution supersedes any requirement of the War Powers Resolution. . . .

Chapter 8. General War

NOTES AND QUESTIONS

1. *War Without the Joint Resolution.* Prior to Congress's approval of the October 16, 2002, joint resolution, some proponents of war on Iraq argued that the President already had the authority to commence it. What theories might support this argument? Are any of these theories suggested by the "whereas" clauses of the eventual joint resolution? United Nations Security Council Resolution 678 and the 1991 Authorization for Use of Military Force in Iraq, cited in those clauses, are reproduced in part at pp. 329-331 of the casebook.

2. *United Nations Involvement.* Unlike the 1991 Gulf War, the 2003 war with Iraq was not conducted with the approval of the United Nations Security Council. But in a resolution passed on November 8, 2002, the Security Council "deplor[ed]" that Iraq had not made full disclosure of or granted the United Nations inspectors unconditional access to its programs and sites for weapons of mass destruction. It found Iraq to be in "material breach of its obligations under relevant resolutions, including resolution 687," but decided to afford Iraq "a final opportunity to comply." S.C. Res. 1441, U.N. Doc. S/RES/1441 (2002). Perhaps most pertinently, the Council "recall[ed] . . . that [it] has repeatedly warned Iraq that it will face serious consequences as a result of its continued violations of its obligations," and it decided to reconvene immediately following any report of future breaches "in order to consider the situation and the need for full compliance." The Administration asserted that this resolution cleared the way for a lawful U.S. attack on Iraq if Iraq failed to comply with its terms. Do you agree? Was a subsequent Security Council resolution necessary to make war with Iraq lawful under international law? Relevant articles of the United Nations Charter are reproduced at pp. 295-297 of the casebook.

3. *The WMD Question.* As of July 2003, U.S. forces in post-war Iraq had located no weapons of mass destruction (WMD), aside from two mobile laboratories of uncertain use. Critics of the war asserted that the Bush administration had misled Congress and the American people, as well as the international community, about the factual predicate for going to war against Iraq, *see, e.g.,* Spencer Ackerman & John B. Judis, *The First Casualty,* New Republic, June 30, 2003, at 14, while defenders of the Administration asserted that the threat of Iraqi WMD had never been the chief reason for the war. Based on the language of the October 16, 2002, joint resolution, how important would you say the WMD threat was in justifying the war? If the critics are right, does it affect the legal authority

Chapter 8. General War 9

conferred by the joint resolution? Compare the debate about the Tonkin Gulf Resolution (casebook p. 263, Note 8). Would we have had the same postwar debate about WMD if President Bush had taken the country to war against Iraq without congressional authorization? Does the controversy suggest that congressional authorizations for war may contribute to political accountability, even if their "whereas" clauses and attendant debate in Congress carry no direct legal effect?

10

Intelligence Operations

C. PROBLEMS IN THE REFORM OF INTELLIGENCE OPERATIONS

2. Executive Branch Reforms

Page 473. Add at the end of Note 5.

The Department of Defense has also developed an Intelligence Support Activity (ISA), created in 1981 to collect intelligence and to conduct covert military operations. Invigorated by Defense Secretary Donald Rumsfeld to participate in the war on terrorism after September 11, the ISA, code-named Gray Fox, now reports to an Under Secretary of Defense for Intelligence. Gray Fox operates independently of the intelligence community. *See* William M. Arkin, *The Secret War: Frustrated by Intelligence Failures, the Defense Department Is Dramatically Expanding Its 'Black World' of Covert Operations*, L.A. Times, Oct. 27, 2002, at M1.

F. THE PRIVATIZATION OF INTELLIGENCE OPERATIONS

2. Dirty Assets

Page 557. Add this new Note.

9. *The Denial-of-Access Claim.* Even though the full D.C. Circuit denied the government's petition for rehearing in *Harbury*, the Supreme

Court granted review and unanimously reversed, Christopher v. Harbury, 536 U.S. 403 (2002). In finding that Harbury's complaint did not state a constitutional denial-of-access claim upon which relief could be granted, the Court declared that an access claim is merely ancillary to an underlying claim, without which a plaintiff cannot have suffered injury by being shut out of court. Thus, the underlying claim must be described in the complaint, and the complaint must identify a remedy that could be awarded and that would not be available in some future lawsuit. In this case, because the acts alleged by Harbury "raise concerns for the separation of powers in trenching on matters committed to other branches," the Court said, it was all the more important for the district court to know whether the denial-of-access allegations stated a claim. The best she could offer, accepted by the Court of Appeals as sufficient, was that she would have brought an action for intentional infliction of emotional distress, and that a lawsuit seeking injunctive relief for that wrong might have saved Bamaca's life. The Supreme Court found Harbury's claim inadequate:

> [E]ven on the assumption that Harbury could surmount all difficulties raised by treating the underlying claim as one for intentional infliction of emotional distress, she could not satisfy the requirement that a backward-looking denial-of-access claim provide a remedy that could not be obtained on an existing claim.

536 U.S. at 420-421.

Harbury's counts naming CIA defendants, including the Guatemalan "asset" who allegedly tortured and killed Bamaca, were among the tort claims that survived the original motion to dismiss in the district court. According to the Supreme Court, Harbury could still seek damages and injunctive relief for emotional distress, although she could not obtain an order that might have saved Bamaca. Her access claim did not support such an order, and it could not compensate her for the loss claimed due to her inability to bring the tort action earlier. What is the likely outcome of the tort claims? What obstacles are most likely to stand in Harbury's way?

11

Organizing for Counterterrorism: An Overview

A. COUNTERING TERRORISM AT HOME AND ABROAD

1. Defining the Terrorist Threat

   a. *What Is Terrorism?*

Page 569. Add this material after Note 6.

People's Mojahedin Organization of Iran v. Department of State

United States Court of Appeals, District of Columbia Circuit, 2003
327 F.3d 1238

SENTELLE, Circuit Judge. The People's Mojahedin Organization of Iran ("PMOI" or "Petitioner") seeks review of 1999 and 2001 decisions of the Secretary of State . . . designating Petitioner as a foreign terrorist organization. . . .

I. Background

We note at the outset that this is PMOI's third petition to this court to review designations of the PMOI as a foreign terrorist organization. *See* People's Mojahedin Org. of Iran v. Dep't. of State, 182 F.3d 17 (D.C. Cir.

1999) ("*PMOI*"); Nat'l Council of Resistance of Iran v. Dep't. of State, 251 F.3d 192 (D.C. Cir. 2001) ("*NCOR*")....

II. Analysis

A. Due Process and Sufficiency of Evidence

Petitioner raises several arguments. First, it contends that its redesignation as a terrorist organization under 8 U.S.C. §1189 is unconstitutional under the Due Process Clause of the Fifth Amendment of the Constitution because the statute permitted the Secretary to rely upon secret evidence – the classified information that respondents refused to disclose and against which PMOI could therefore not effectively defend. We reject this contention.... [T]hat statute authorizes designation of a foreign terrorist organization when the Secretary finds three elements. As to the first, that is that the organization is a foreign organization, there is not and cannot be any dispute. The People's Mojahedin is so assuredly a foreign organization that until the Secretary's designation of the NCOR as its alias, it could not even establish a presence in the United States. Nothing has changed in that regard since our prior decisions on the subject.

As to the second element, the PMOI advances a colorable argument: that the Secretary was able under §1189(a)(3)(B) to "consider classified information in making [this designation]" and that the classified information was not "subject to disclosure" except to the court ex parte and in camera for purposes of this judicial review. Petitioner contends that this violates the due process standard set forth in Abourezk v. Reagan, 785 F.2d 1043, 1061 (D.C. Cir. 1986), "that a court may not dispose of the merits of a case on the basis of ex parte, in camera submissions." While colorable, this argument will not carry the day.

First, we have already set forth in *NCOR* the due process standards that the Secretary must meet in making designations under the statute. We held that the Constitution requires the Secretary in designating foreign terrorist organizations to provide to the potential designees, "notice that the designation is impending." *NCOR*, 251 F.3d at 208. We further required that the Secretary must afford the potential designee an "opportunity to be heard at a meaningful time and in a meaningful manner." *Id.* at 209. The record reflects that the Secretary complied with our instructions.

Granted, petitioners argue that their opportunity to be heard was not meaningful, given that the Secretary relied on secret information to which they were not afforded access. The response to this is twofold. We already decided in *NCOR* that due process required the disclosure of only the

Chapter 11. Organizing for Counterterrorism: An Overview 15

unclassified portions of the administrative record. 251 F.3d at 207-09. We made that determination informed by the historically recognized proposition that under the separation of powers created by the United States Constitution, the Executive Branch has control and responsibility over access to classified information and has "'compelling interest' in withholding national security information from unauthorized persons in the course of executive business." Dep't. of the Navy v. Egan, 484 U.S. 518, 527 (1988) (quoting Snepp v. United States, 444 U.S. 507, 509 n. 3 (1980)). In the context of another statutory scheme involving classified information, we noted the courts are often ill-suited to determine the sensitivity of classified information. United States v. Yunis, 867 F.2d 617, 623 (D.C. Cir. 1989) ("Things that did not make sense to [a judge] would make all too much sense to a foreign counter intelligence specialist. . . ."). The Due Process Clause requires only that process which is due under the circumstances of the case. We have already established in *NCOR* the process which is due under the circumstances of this sensitive matter of classified intelligence in the effort to combat foreign terrorism. The Secretary has complied with the standard we set forth therein, and nothing further is due.

However, even if we err in describing the process due, even had the Petitioner been entitled to have its counsel or itself view the classified information, the breach of that entitlement has caused it no harm. This brings us to Petitioner's statutory objection. Petitioner argues that there is not adequate record support for the Secretary's determination that it is a foreign terrorist organization under the statute. However, on this element, even the unclassified record taken alone is quite adequate to support the Secretary's determination. Indeed, as to this element – that is, that the organization engages in terrorist activities – the People's Mojahedin has effectively admitted not only the adequacy of the unclassified record, but the truth of the allegation. . . .

By its own admission, the PMOI has

> (1) attacked with mortars the Islamic Revolutionary Prosecutor's Office; (2) assassinated a former Iranian prosecutor and killed his security guards; (3) killed the Deputy Chief of the Iranian Joint Staff Command, who was the personal military adviser to Supreme Leader Khamenei; (4) attacked with mortars the Iranian Central Command Headquarters of the Islamic Revolutionary Guard Corps and the Defense Industries Organization in Tehran; (5) attacked and targeted with mortars the offices of the Iranian Supreme Leader Khamenei, and of the head of the State Exigencies Council; (6) attacked with mortars the central headquarters of the

Revolutionary Guards; (7) attacked with mortars two Revolutionary Guards Corps headquarters; and (8) attacked the headquarters of the Iranian State Security Forces in Tehran.

Were there no classified information in the file, we could hardly find that the Secretary's determination that the Petitioner engaged in terrorist activities is "lacking substantial support in the administrative record taken as a whole," even without repairing to the "classified information submitted to the court." 8 U.S.C. §1189(b)(3)(D). . . .

The remaining element under §1189(a)(1) is that "the terrorist activity or terrorism of the organization threatens the security of United States nationals or the national security of the United States." *Id.* §1189(a)(1)(C). The thrust of Petitioner's argument is that its allegedly terrorist acts were not acts of terrorism under the statute, because they do not meet the requirement of subsection (C). Petitioner argues that the attempt to overthrow the despotic government of Iran, which itself remains on the State Department's list of state sponsors of terrorism, is not "terrorist activity," or if it is, that it does not threaten the security of the United States or its nationals. We cannot review that claim. In PMOI we expressly held that that finding "is nonjusticiable." 182 F.3d at 23. As we stated in that decision, "it is beyond the judicial function for a court to review foreign policy decisions of the Executive Branch." *Id.* (citing Chicago & Southern Air Lines v. Waterman Steamship Corp., 333 U.S. 103, 111 (1948)). . . . In short, we find neither statutory nor due process errors in the Secretary's designation of petitioner as a foreign terrorist organization.

B. Petitioner's Other Claims

Petitioner raises several other arguments to the effect that the designation violates its constitutional rights. Those warranting separate discussion fall under the general heading of First Amendment claims. Petitioner's argument that its First Amendment rights have been violated rests on the consequences of the designation. Petitioner argues that by forbidding all persons within or subject to the jurisdiction of the United States from "knowingly provid[ing] material support or resources," 18 U.S.C. §2339B(a)(1), to it as a designated foreign terrorist organization, the statute violates its rights of free speech and association guaranteed by the First Amendment. We disagree.

As the Ninth Circuit held in Humanitarian Law Project v. Reno, 205 F.3d 1130, 1135 (9th Cir. 2000) [casebook p. 832], the statute "is not aimed at interfering with the expressive component of [the organization's] conduct

Chapter 11. Organizing for Counterterrorism: An Overview

but at stopping aid to terrorist groups." It is conduct and not communication that the statute controls. We join the Ninth Circuit in observing that "there is no constitutional right to facilitate terrorism by giving terrorists the weapons and explosives with which to carry out their grisly missions. Nor, of course, is there a right to provide resources with which terrorists can buy weapons and explosives." *Id.* at 1133. . . .

III. Conclusion

For the reasons set forth above, we conclude that in the designation and redesignation of the People's Mojahedin of Iran as a foreign terrorist organization, the Secretary of State afforded all the process that the organization was due, and that this designation violated neither statutory nor constitutional rights of the Petitioner. We therefore deny the petitions for review.

So ordered.

EDWARDS, J., concurring [omitted].

NOTES AND QUESTIONS

1. *Process Without Access?* If PMOI is entitled to the protections of the Due Process Clause, how can the process due include denying to PMOI access to the evidence upon which their designation is based? On what basis did the court justify a process that was admittedly not "meaningful"?

2. *Result-Oriented?* The consequences of designation are dire, as the court noted in its 2001 decision, casebook p. 566. Under the circumstances, why do you suppose the process obligations of the government are so scant? Would you say that the outcome in PMOI was determined primarily by the State Department, Congress, or the court?

3. *The Statutory Argument.* Are you persuaded by PMOI's statutory argument? Why should the statutory question be any less amenable to judicial resolution than the constitutional claim?

4. *First Amendment Issues.* The First Amendment consequences of designation are explored at casebook pp. 826-840.

2. Planning for Homeland Security

Page 582. Add this material before the Notes and Questions.

In July 2002, the Office of Homeland Security published the National Strategy for Homeland Security, *available at http://www.whitehouse.gov/homeland*. The document outlined the structure and functions of a proposed Department of Homeland Security (DHS). In November 2002, the new department was authorized in the Homeland Security Act of 2002, Pub. L. No. 107-296, 116 Stat. 2135 (2002). The Act merges all or part of 22 agencies and 170,000 employees into the DHS, and it charges the new Department with analyzing terrorist threats, guarding borders and airports, protecting critical infrastructure, and coordinating the response to future terrorist emergencies. Apart from creating the DHS, the Act contains information-sharing and access to information provisions noted in this Supplement for Chapters 12 and 15, *infra*.

12
Investigating Terrorism and Other National Security Threats

B. THE FOURTH AMENDMENT FRAMEWORK

4. Investigations Abroad

Page 650. Add this material at the end of Note 5.

Even if the Fifth Amendment applied to acts of U.S. agents against aliens abroad, it is not certain that it protects against investigatory torture. In Chavez v. Martinez, 123 S. Ct. 1994 (2003), a badly fractured Supreme Court ruled on claims of liability asserted by a plaintiff who had been subjected to persistent police questioning while he was in the hospital incapacitated by extreme pain. Five members voted to remand the question whether he could pursue a claim for violation of his substantive due process rights, but the Court could not agree about the scope and applicability of those rights or the related right against self-incrimination.

Three justices joined in part of an opinion by Justice Thomas asserting that the interrogation was not egregious or conscience-shocking enough to violate the plaintiff's substantive due process rights. They reasoned that "freedom from unwanted police questioning is [not] a right so fundamental that it cannot be abridged absent a 'compelling state interest.'" *Id.* at 2006. For them, it was enough that the questioning was justified by *some* government interest – here the need to preserve critical evidence concerning a shooting by a police officer – and that it was not "conduct intended to injure in some way unjustifiable by any government interest." *Id.* at 2005.

Justice Stevens concluded that "the interrogation of respondent was the functional equivalent of an attempt to obtain an involuntary confession from a prisoner by torturous methods," which is "a classic example of a violation of a constitutional right 'implicit in the concept of ordered liberty.'" *Id.* at 2010 (Stevens, J., concurring in part, dissenting in part).

Justice Kennedy (joined on this point by Justices Stevens and Ginsburg) agreed that the use of investigatory torture violates a person's fundamental right to liberty, but noted that interrogating suspects who are in pain or anguish is not necessarily torture when the police have "legitimate reasons, borne of exigency, . . . [such as] [l]ocating the victim of a kidnapping, ascertaining the whereabouts of a dangerous assailant or accomplice, or determining whether there is a rogue police officer." *Id.* at 2017 (Kennedy, J., concurring in part, dissenting in part). On the other hand, he added, the police may not prolong or increase the suspect's suffering or threaten to do so to elicit a statement. The test for a constitutional violation, in Justice Kennedy's view, was whether the police "exploited" the suspect's pain to secure his statement. He found that they had done so in *Chavez*.

Under any of the foregoing tests would torture in the United States of a suspected terrorist in order to obtain information needed to prevent an imminent terrorist attack violate substantive due process?

C. CONGRESSIONAL AUTHORITY FOR SURVEILLANCE: THE FOREIGN INTELLIGENCE SURVEILLANCE ACT

Page 679. Add this material at the end of Note 2.b.

Why doesn't a pen register installed by the telephone company at the FBI's request violate the Fourth Amendment? In Smith v. Maryland, 442 U.S. 735 (1979), the Supreme Court explained that people do not have any actual or legitimate expectation of privacy in the numbers that they dial, because they voluntarily convey that information to the phone company and therefore assume the risk that the phone company will reveal the dialed numbers to the police. The installation of a pen register, consequently, was not a search. The Court emphasized, however, that pen registers do not record the contents of telephone communications. *Id.* at 741.

Chapter 12. Investigating Terrorism 21

Page 679. Add this material at the end of Note 2.c.

Recall that Smith v. Maryland, upholding the constitutionality of the pen register, emphasized that pen registers do not record the contents of telephone communications. See prior note, this Supplement. Is *Smith* authority for searching e-mail subject lines and URLs without a warrant?

Page 679. Replace Note 2.d. with this material.

In United States v. Miller, 425 U.S. 435 (1976), the Supreme Court held that police seizure of bank records under a defective subpoena duces tecum was lawful because the person to whom they pertained had no protected Fourth Amendment privacy interest in checks, deposit slips, and other financial information voluntarily conveyed to banks. "The depositor takes the risk, in revealing his affairs to another, that the information will be conveyed by that person to the Government." *Id.* at 443. When the government demands such information from a bank by subpoena, its demand is subject only to the unexacting requirements that the demand not be indefinite or overbroad, and that it be relevant to an inquiry which the agency is authorized to make. *Id.* at 446.

Prior to September 11, FISA authorized the FISC to issue an order for production of certain transactional records from a third-party custodian if the government certified that it had "reason to believe that the person to whom the records pertain is a foreign power or an agent of a foreign power." 50 U.S.C. §1862 (2000). The same standard applied to "national security letters," which the FBI itself is authorized by statute to issue directly to third-party record custodians, such as banks and telephone companies, for production of various transactional records. *See* Right to Financial Privacy Act, 12 U.S.C. §3414(a)(5)(A) (financial records); Fair Credit Reporting Act, 15 U.S.C. §§1681u(a) & (c) (consumer credit information); Electronic Communications Privacy Act, 18 U.S.C. §2709 (electronic communication transactional records). *See also* 50 U.S.C. §436(a)(2)(B)(i) ("is, or may be, disclosing classified information in an unauthorized manner to a foreign power or agent of a foreign power") (financial records, consumer reports, travel records of persons with access to classified information). National security letters have been described as "the intelligence corollary to . . . administrative subpoena[s]." Lee S. Strickland, *New Information-Related Laws and the Impact on Civil Liberties, http://www.asis.org/Bulletin/Mar-02/strickland2.html.*

The USA PATRIOT Act broadened both the scope of and the standard for FISA orders and national security letters. The orders can now be used for the production of "tangible things (including books, records, papers, documents, and other items) for an investigation to collect foreign intelligence information not concerning a United States person or to protect against international terrorism or clandestine intelligence activities, provided that such investigation of a United States person is not conducted solely upon the basis of activities protected by the first amendment to the Constitution." See 50 U.S.C. §1861(a)(1), as amended by Pub. L. No. 107-108, §314(a)(6), 115 Stat. 1394, 1401 (2001). The Act also adopted the investigation-to-protect-against-international-terrorism standard for national security letters. Pub. L. No. 107-56, §505, 115 Stat. 272, 364 (2001). Which standard – the old FISA standard or the new USA PATRIOT Act standard – is more lenient? Consider the following assessment.

> Previously, the FBI could get the credit card records of anyone suspected of being a foreign agent. Under the PATRIOT Act, broadly read, the FBI can get the entire database of the credit card company. Under prior law, the FBI could get library borrowing records only with a subpoena in a criminal investigation, and generally had to ask for the records of a specific patron. Under the PATRIOT Act, broadly read, the FBI can go into a public library and ask for the records on everybody who ever used the library, or who used it on a certain day, or who checked out certain kinds of books. It can do the same at any bank, telephone company, hotel or motel, hospital, or university – merely upon the claim that the information is . . . sought for . . . an investigation to protect against international terrorism or clandestine intelligence activities.

Terrorism Investigations and the Constitution: Hearing Before the Subcomm. on the Constitution of the House Comm. on the Judiciary, 2003 WL 21153545 (2003) (statement of James X. Dempsey, Executive Director, Center for Democracy & Technology). Should the USA PATRIOT Act be so "broadly read"? Can you read it any other way? Does the Constitution compel a narrower reading on the theory of avoiding an unnecessary constitutional (here Fourth Amendment) question? If so, what is it?

Theoretically, both subpoenas duces tecum and FISA orders for the production of tangible things are subject to some judicial supervision. Subpoenas for bank records, for example, may be issued by some agencies, but they can be challenged in court by the bank's motion to quash or limit. FISA orders for production of tangible things are issued only if the government certifies in an application to the FISC that the order complies with the applicable standard. *See* 50 U.S.C. §1861(c)(1). One scholar has argued about such orders that "it is not readily conceivable that a federal judge would issue . . . a broad order without inquiry into the validity of the

Chapter 12. Investigating Terrorism 23

relevance certification and substantial details as to how the government would justify collection of information on persons unrelated to the investigation." Strickland, *supra*. But the government itself suggests that the FISC's role is simply to ascertain that the government has made the required certification, not whether the certification is justified. *See* Letter from Jamie E. Brown, Acting Asst. Attorney General, Office of Legislative Affairs, U.S. Department of Justice, to F. James Sensenbrenner, Jr., Chair, Committee on the Judiciary, U.S. House of Representatives (May 13, 2003) [hereinafter Brown], at 3.

National security letters, on the other hand, escape all judicial supervision. In Burrows v. Superior Court, 529 P.2d 590 (Cal. 1974), the California Supreme Court held that a search of bank records pursuant to an "informal" police request was unlawful. The United States Supreme Court subsequently distinguished *Burrows* in approving a search of bank records pursuant to a defective subpoena in *Miller* by emphasizing that a subpoena involved "'compulsion by legal process,'" not a mere "'informal oral request for information.'" 425 U.S. at 445 n. 7 (quoting *Burrows*, 529 P.2d at 593). Does this distinction afford any basis for challenging the constitutionality of national security letters, as distinct from subpoenas or FISC orders for transactional records? Even if it does not, is there any reason to be more concerned about abuse of such letters than of FISA orders or subpoenas?

Of course this question presupposes a challenger. In fact, third-party document custodians are forbidden from disclosing the existence of the national security letter to the most probable challenger – the person to whom the transactional records pertain. This may account for the fact that there have been no reported legal challenges to national security letters. *See* Brown, *supra*, at 4. Since the USA PATRIOT Act, the volume of national security letters issued by the government has apparently increased dramatically, *see* Dan Eggen & Robert O'Harrow, Jr., *U.S. Steps Up Secret Surveillance*, Wash. Post, March 24, 2003, at A1, but the government has successfully resisted Freedom of Information Act requests for the numbers. *See* American Civil Liberties Union v. United States Dept. of Justice, 2003 WL 21152857 (D.D.C. 2003).

Page 687. Add this material at the end of Note 9.

The Intelligence Authorization Act for Fiscal Year 2002, Pub. L. No. 107-108, §314(a)(2)(B) & (4), 115 Stat. 1394, 1402 (2001), also extended from 24 to 72 hours the time the Attorney General has to authorize surveillance or searches before review by the FISC. 50 U.S.C. §§1805(f),

1824(e). Between 1978 and September 11, 2001, Attorneys General issued 47 emergency authorizations under FISA. Between September 11, 2001, and September 19, 2002, the Attorney General authorized 113 wiretaps and/or physical searches under FISA. Brown, *supra,* at 17-18.

Section 225 of the Homeland Security Act expands the circumstances in which law enforcement can use pen registers and trap and trace devices without seeking a court order to include emergencies involving "an immediate threat to a national security interest." Pub. L. No. 107-296, §225(i)(3)(c), 116 Stat. 2135, 2158 (2002). Under the same section, an Internet service provider may disclose the content of electronic communications to any government agency if the ISP in "good faith" believes that the communication relates to information that involves the risk of death or serious physical injury. *Id.* §225(d)(1)(d). How, if at all, do these authorities exacerbate the judicial review and monitoring problems noted in the text?

Page 691. Add this material after Note 11.d.

In re: Sealed Case No. 02-001, 02-002
Foreign Intelligence Surveillance Court of Review, 2002
310 F.3d 717

GUY, Senior Circuit Judge, presiding; SILBERMAN and LEAVY, Senior Circuit Judges.

PER CURIAM: This is the first appeal from the Foreign Intelligence Surveillance Court to the Court of Review since the passage of the Foreign Intelligence Surveillance Act (FISA), 50 U.S.C. §§1801-1862 (West 1991 and Supp. 2002), in 1978. The appeal is brought by the United States from a FISA court surveillance order which imposed certain restrictions on the government. . . .

I.

The court's decision from which the government appeals imposed certain requirements and limitations accompanying an order authorizing electronic surveillance of an "agent of a foreign power" as defined in FISA. There is no disagreement between the government and the FISA court as to the propriety of the electronic surveillance . . . . [T]he court ordered that

Chapter 12. Investigating Terrorism

law enforcement officials shall not make recommendations to intelligence officials concerning the initiation, operation, continuation or expansion of FISA searches or surveillances. Additionally, the FBI and the Criminal Division [of the Department of Justice] shall ensure that law enforcement officials do not direct or control the use of the FISA procedures to enhance criminal prosecution, and that advice intended to preserve the option of a criminal prosecution does not inadvertently result in the Criminal Division's directing or controlling the investigation using FISA searches and surveillances toward law enforcement objectives.

To ensure the Justice Department followed these strictures the court also fashioned what the government refers to as a "chaperone requirement"; that a unit of the Justice Department, the Office of Intelligence Policy and Review (OIPR) (composed of 31 lawyers and 25 support staff), "be invited" to all meetings between the FBI and the Criminal Division involving consultations for the purpose of coordinating efforts "to investigate or protect against foreign attack or other grave hostile acts, sabotage, international terrorism, or clandestine intelligence activities by foreign powers or their agents." If representatives of OIPR are unable to attend such meetings, "OIPR shall be appri[s]ed of the substance of the meetings forthwith in writing so that the Court may be notified at the earliest opportunity."

These restrictions are not original to the order appealed. They were actually set forth in an opinion written by the former Presiding Judge of the FISA court on May 17 of this year. [*See* In re All Matters Submitted to the Foreign Intelligence Surveillance Court, 218 F. Supp. 2d 611 (2002).] . . .

We think it fair to say, however, that the May 17 opinion of the FISA court does not clearly set forth the basis for its decision. It appears to proceed from the assumption that FISA constructed a barrier between counterintelligence/intelligence officials and law enforcement officers in the Executive Branch – indeed, it uses the word "wall" popularized by certain commentators (and journalists) to describe that supposed barrier.

The "wall" emerges from the court's implicit interpretation of FISA. The court apparently believes it can approve applications for electronic surveillance only if the government's objective is *not* primarily directed toward criminal prosecution of the foreign agents for their foreign intelligence activity. But the court neither refers to any FISA language supporting that view, nor does it reference the Patriot Act amendments, which the government contends specifically altered FISA to make clear that an application could be obtained even if criminal prosecution is the primary counter mechanism.

Instead the court relied for its imposition of the disputed restrictions on its statutory authority to approve "minimization procedures" designed to prevent the acquisition, retention, and dissemination within the government of material gathered in an electronic surveillance that is unnecessary to the government's need for foreign intelligence information. 50 U.S.C. §1801(h). . . .

II.

The government makes two main arguments. The first . . . is that the supposed pre-Patriot Act limitation in FISA that restricts the government's intention to use foreign intelligence information in criminal prosecutions is an illusion; it finds no support in either the language of FISA or its legislative history. The government does recognize that several courts of appeals, while upholding the use of FISA surveillances, have opined that FISA may be used only if the government's primary purpose in pursuing foreign intelligence information is not criminal prosecution, but the government argues that those decisions, which did not carefully analyze the statute, were incorrect in their statements, if not incorrect in their holdings.

Alternatively, the government contends that even if the primary purpose test was a legitimate construction of FISA prior to the passage of the Patriot Act, that Act's amendments to FISA eliminate that concept. And as a corollary, the government insists the FISA court's construction of the minimization procedures is far off the mark both because it is a misconstruction of those provisions *per se*, as well as an end run around the specific amendments in the Patriot Act designed to deal with the real issue underlying this case. The government, moreover, contends that the FISA court's restrictions, which the court described as minimization procedures, are so intrusive into the operation of the Department of Justice as to exceed the constitutional authority of Article III judges.

The government's brief, and its supplementary brief requested by this court, also set forth its view that the primary purpose test is not required by the Fourth Amendment. . . .

The 1978 FISA

We turn first to the statute as enacted in 1978. . . . [The court reviewed the definitions of "foreign intelligence information" and "agent of a foreign power" and noted that each is concerned with national security crimes.]

In light of these definitions, it is quite puzzling that the Justice Department, at some point during the 1980s, began to read the statute as limiting the Department's ability to obtain FISA orders if it intended to

Chapter 12. Investigating Terrorism 27

prosecute the targeted agents – even for foreign intelligence crimes. To be sure, section 1804, which sets forth the elements of an application for an order, required a national security official in the Executive Branch – typically the Director of the FBI – to certify that "the purpose" of the surveillance is to obtain foreign intelligence information (amended by the Patriot Act to read "a significant purpose"). But as the government now argues, the definition of foreign intelligence information includes evidence of crimes such as espionage, sabotage or terrorism. Indeed, it is virtually impossible to read the 1978 FISA to exclude from its purpose the prosecution of foreign intelligence crimes, most importantly because, as we have noted, the definition of an agent of a foreign power – if he or she is a U.S. person – is grounded on criminal conduct.

It does not seem that FISA, at least as originally enacted, even contemplated that the FISA court would inquire into the government's purpose in seeking foreign intelligence information. Section 1805, governing the standards a FISA court judge is to use in determining whether to grant a surveillance order, requires the judge to find that

> the application which has been filed contains all statements and certifications required by section 1804 of this title and, if the target is a United States person, the certification or certifications are not clearly erroneous on the basis of the statement made under section 1804(a)(7)(E) of this title and any other information furnished under section 1804(d) of this title.

50 U.S.C. §1805(a)(5). And section 1804(a)(7)(E) requires that the application include "a statement of the basis of the certification that – (i) the information sought is the type of foreign intelligence information designated; and (ii) such information cannot reasonably be obtained by normal investigative techniques." That language certainly suggests that, aside from the probable cause, identification of facilities, and minimization procedures the judge is to determine and approve (also set forth in section 1805), the only other issues are whether electronic surveillance is necessary to obtain the information and whether the information sought is actually foreign intelligence information – not the government's proposed use of that information.

Nor does the legislative history cast doubt on the obvious reading of the statutory language that foreign intelligence information includes evidence of foreign intelligence crimes. . . .

The government argues persuasively that arresting and prosecuting terrorist agents of, or spies for, a foreign power may well be the best technique to prevent them from successfully continuing their terrorist or espionage activity. The government might wish to surveil the agent for some period of time to discover other participants in a conspiracy or to uncover a foreign power's plans, but typically at some point the government would wish to apprehend the agent and it might be that only a prosecution would provide sufficient incentives for the agent to cooperate with the government. . . .

Congress was concerned about the government's use of FISA surveillance to obtain information not truly intertwined with the government's efforts to protect against threats from foreign powers. Accordingly, the certification of purpose under section 1804(a)(7)(B) served to

> prevent the practice of targeting, for example, a foreign power for electronic surveillance when the true purpose of the surveillance is to gather information about an individual for other than foreign intelligence purposes. It is also designed to make explicit that the sole purpose of such surveillance is to secure "foreign intelligence information," as defined, and not to obtain some other type of information.

[H.R. Rep. No. 95-1283 (hereinafter "H. Rep.")] at 76; *see also* [S. Rep. No. 95-701 (hereinafter "S. Rep.")] at 51. But Congress did not impose any restrictions on the government's use of the foreign intelligence information to prosecute agents of foreign powers for foreign intelligence crimes. Admittedly, the House, at least in one statement, noted that FISA surveillances "are not primarily for the purpose of gathering evidence of a crime. They are to obtain foreign intelligence information, which when it concerns United States persons must be necessary to important national concerns." H. Rep. at 36. That, however, was an observation, not a proscription. And the House as well as the Senate made clear that prosecution is one way to combat foreign intelligence crimes. *See id.*; S. Rep. at 10-11.

The origin of what the government refers to as the false dichotomy between foreign intelligence information that is evidence of foreign intelligence crimes and that which is not appears to have been a Fourth Circuit case decided in 1980. United States v. Truong Dinh Hung, 629 F.2d 908 (4th Cir. 1980). That case, however, involved an electronic surveillance carried out prior to the passage of FISA and predicated on the President's executive power. In approving the district court's exclusion of evidence obtained through a warrantless surveillance subsequent to the point in time when the government's investigation became "primarily" driven by law enforcement objectives, the court held that the Executive Branch should be excused from securing a warrant only when "the object of the search or the surveillance is a foreign power, its agents or collaborators," and "the surveillance is conducted 'primarily' for foreign intelligence reasons." *Id.* at 915. . . .

[S]ome time in the 1980s – the exact moment is shrouded in historical mist – the Department [of Justice] applied the *Truong* analysis to an interpretation of the FISA statute. What is clear is that in 1995 the Attorney General adopted "Procedures for Contacts Between the FBI and the Criminal Division Concerning Foreign Intelligence and Foreign Counterintelligence Investigations."

Apparently to avoid running afoul of the primary purpose test used by some courts, the 1995 Procedures limited contacts between the FBI and the Criminal Division in cases where FISA surveillance or searches were being conducted by the FBI for foreign intelligence (FI) or foreign counterintelligence (FCI) purposes. The procedures state that "the FBI and Criminal Division should ensure that advice intended to preserve the option of a criminal prosecution does not inadvertently result in either the fact or the appearance of the Criminal Division's *directing or controlling* the FI or FCI investigation toward law enforcement objectives." 1995 Procedures at 2, ¶6 (emphasis added). Although these procedures provided for significant information sharing and coordination between criminal and FI or FCI investigations, based at least in part on the "directing or controlling" language, they eventually came to be narrowly interpreted within the Department of Justice, and most particularly by OIPR, as requiring OIPR to act as a "wall" to prevent the FBI intelligence officials from communicating with the Criminal Division regarding ongoing FI or FCI investigations. . . .

The Department's attitude changed somewhat after the May 2000 report by the Attorney General . . . concluded that the Department's concern over how the FISA court or other federal courts might interpret the primary purpose test has inhibited necessary coordination between intelligence and law enforcement officials. *See id.* at 721-34. . . . [T]he Attorney General, in January 2000, issued additional, interim procedures designed to address coordination problems identified in that report. In August 2001, the Deputy Attorney General issued a memorandum clarifying Department of Justice policy governing intelligence sharing and establishing additional requirements. (These actions, however, did not replace the 1995 Procedures.) . . .

The Patriot Act and the FISA Court's Decision

The passage of the Patriot Act altered and to some degree muddied the landscape. In October 2001, Congress amended FISA to change "the purpose" language in 1804(a)(7)(B) to "a significant purpose." It also added a provision allowing "Federal officers who conduct electronic surveillance to acquire foreign intelligence information" to "consult with Federal law enforcement officers to coordinate efforts to investigate or protect against" attack or other grave hostile acts, sabotage or international terrorism, or clandestine intelligence activities, by foreign powers or their agents. 50 U.S.C. §1806(k)(1). And such coordination "shall not preclude" the government's certification that a significant purpose of the surveillance is to obtain foreign intelligence information, or the issuance of an order authorizing the surveillance. *Id.* §1806(k)(2). Although the Patriot Act amendments to FISA expressly sanctioned consultation and coordination between intelligence and law enforcement officials, in response to the first applications filed by OIPR under those amendments, in November 2001, the FISA court for the first time adopted the 1995 Procedures, as augmented by the January 2000 and August 2001 Procedures, as "minimization procedures" to apply in all cases before the court.

The Attorney General interpreted the Patriot Act quite differently. On March 6, 2002, the Attorney General approved new "Intelligence Sharing Procedures" to implement the Act's amendments to FISA. The 2002 Procedures supersede prior procedures and were designed to permit the complete exchange of information and advice between intelligence and law enforcement officials. They eliminated the "direction and control" test and allowed the exchange of advice between the FBI, OIPR, and the Criminal Division regarding "the initiation, operation, continuation, or expansion of FISA searches or surveillance." On March 7, 2002, the government filed a motion with the FISA court, noting that the Department of Justice had adopted the 2002 Procedures and proposing to follow those procedures in all matters before the court. The government also asked the FISA court to vacate its orders adopting the prior procedures as minimization procedures in all cases and imposing special "wall" procedures in certain cases.

Unpersuaded by the Attorney General's interpretation of the Patriot Act, the court ordered that the 2002 Procedures be adopted, *with modifications*, as minimization procedures to apply in all cases. The court emphasized that the definition of minimization procedures had not been amended by the Patriot Act, and reasoned that the 2002 Procedures "cannot be used by the government to amend the Act in ways Congress has not." . . .

Undeterred, the government submitted the application at issue in this

Chapter 12. Investigating Terrorism 31

appeal on July 19, 2002, and expressly proposed using the 2002 Procedures *without modification*. In an order issued the same day, the FISA judge hearing the application granted an order for surveillance of the target but modified the 2002 Procedures consistent with the court's May 17, 2002 *en banc* order. It is the July 19, 2002 order that the government appeals . . . .

Essentially, the FISA court took portions of the Attorney General's augmented 1995 Procedures – adopted to deal with the primary purpose standard – and imposed them generically as minimization procedures. In doing so, the FISA court erred. It did not provide any constitutional basis for its action – we think there is none – and misconstrued the main statutory provision on which it relied. The court mistakenly categorized the augmented 1995 Procedures as FISA minimization procedures and then compelled the government to utilize a modified version of those procedures in a way that is clearly inconsistent with the statutory purpose.

Under section 1805 of FISA, "the judge shall enter an ex parte order as requested or as modified approving the electronic surveillance if he finds that . . . the proposed minimization procedures meet the definition of minimization procedures under section 1801(h) of this title." 50 U.S.C. §1805(a)(4). [Section 1801(h)] defines minimization procedures in pertinent part as:

> (1) specific procedures, which shall be adopted by the Attorney General, that are reasonably designed in light of the purpose and technique of the particular surveillance, to minimize the acquisition and retention, and prohibit the dissemination, of nonpublicly available information concerning unconsenting United States persons consistent with the need of the United States to obtain, produce, and disseminate foreign intelligence information; . . .

. . . [M]inimization procedures are designed to protect, as far as reasonable, against the acquisition, retention, and dissemination of nonpublic information which is not foreign intelligence information. If the data is not foreign intelligence information as defined by the statute, the procedures are to ensure that the government does not use the information to identify the target or third party, unless such identification is necessary to properly understand or assess the foreign intelligence information that is collected. *Id.* §1801(h)(2). . . .

The minimization procedures allow, however, the retention and dissemination of non-foreign intelligence information which is evidence of *ordinary crimes* for preventative or prosecutorial purposes. *See* 50 U.S.C. §1801(h)(3). Therefore, if through interceptions or searches, evidence of "a serious crime totally unrelated to intelligence matters" is incidentally acquired, the evidence is *"not* . . . required to be destroyed." H. Rep. at 62 (emphasis added). As we have explained, under the 1978 Act, "evidence of certain crimes like espionage would itself constitute 'foreign intelligence information,' as defined, because it is necessary to protect against clandestine intelligence activities by foreign powers or their agents." H. Rep. at 62; *see also id.* at 49. In light of these purposes of the minimization procedures, there is simply no basis for the FISA court's reliance on section 1801(h) to limit criminal prosecutors' ability to advise FBI intelligence officials on the initiation, operation, continuation, or expansion of FISA surveillances to obtain foreign intelligence information, even if such information includes evidence of a foreign intelligence crime.

The FISA court's decision and order not only misinterpreted and misapplied minimization procedures it was entitled to impose, but as the government argues persuasively, the FISA court may well have exceeded the constitutional bounds that restrict an Article III court. The FISA court asserted authority to govern the internal organization and investigative procedures of the Department of Justice which are the province of the Executive Branch (Article II) and the Congress (Article I). Subject to statutes dealing with the organization of the Justice Department, however, the Attorney General has the responsibility to determine how to deploy personnel resources. . . .

We also think the refusal by the FISA court to consider the legal significance of the Patriot Act's crucial amendments was error. The government, in order to avoid the requirement of meeting the "primary purpose" test, specifically sought an amendment to section 1804(a)(7)(B) which had required a certification "that the purpose of the surveillance is to obtain foreign intelligence information" so as to delete the article "the" before "purpose" and replace it with "a." The government made perfectly clear to Congress why it sought the legislative change. Congress, although accepting the government's explanation for the need for the amendment, adopted language which it perceived as not giving the government quite the degree of modification it wanted. Accordingly, section 1804(a)(7)(B)'s wording became "that a *significant* purpose of the surveillance is to obtain foreign intelligence information" (emphasis added). There is simply no question, however, that Congress was keenly aware that this amendment relaxed a requirement that the government show that its primary purpose was other than criminal prosecution. . . .

. . . [T]here can be no doubt as to Congress' intent in amending section 1804(a)(7)(B). Indeed, it went further to emphasize its purpose in breaking down barriers between criminal law enforcement and intelligence (or counterintelligence) gathering by adding section 1806(k):

Chapter 12. Investigating Terrorism

(k) Consultation with Federal law enforcement officer

(1) Federal officers who conduct electronic surveillance to acquire foreign intelligence information under this title may consult with Federal law enforcement officers to coordinate efforts to investigate or protect against

(A) actual or potential attack or other grave hostile acts of a foreign power or an agent of a foreign power; or

(B) sabotage or international terrorism by a foreign power or an agent of a foreign power; or

(C) clandestine intelligence activities by an intelligence service or network of a foreign power or by an agent of a foreign power.

(2) Coordination authorized under paragraph (1) shall not preclude the certification required by section [1804](a)(7)(B) of this title or the entry of an order under section [1805] of this title. . . .

. . . [W]hen Congress explicitly authorizes consultation and coordination between different offices in the government, without even suggesting a limitation on who is to direct and control, it necessarily implies that either could be taking the lead. . . .

Accordingly, the Patriot Act amendments clearly disapprove the primary purpose test. And as a matter of straightforward logic, if a FISA application can be granted even if "foreign intelligence" is only a significant – not a primary – purpose, another purpose can be primary. One other legitimate purpose that could exist is to prosecute a target for a foreign intelligence crime. . . .

. . . [I]t is our task to do our best to read the statute to honor congressional intent. The better reading, it seems to us, excludes from the purpose of gaining foreign intelligence information a sole objective of criminal prosecution. We therefore reject the government's argument to the contrary. Yet this may not make much practical difference. Because, as the government points out, when it commences an electronic surveillance of a foreign agent, typically it will not have decided whether to prosecute the agent (whatever may be the subjective intent of the investigators or lawyers who initiate an investigation). So long as the government entertains a realistic option of dealing with the agent other than through criminal prosecution, it satisfies the significant purpose test.

The important point is – and here we agree with the government – the Patriot Act amendment, by using the word "significant," eliminated any justification for the FISA court to balance the relative weight the government places on criminal prosecution as compared to other counterintelligence responses. If the certification of the application's purpose articulates a broader objective than criminal prosecution – such as stopping an ongoing conspiracy – and includes other potential non-prosecutorial responses, the government meets the statutory test. Of course, if the court concluded that the government's sole objective was merely to gain evidence of past criminal conduct – even foreign intelligence crimes – to punish the agent rather than halt ongoing espionage or terrorist activity, the application should be denied.

. . . It can be argued, however, that by providing that an application is to be granted if the government has only a "significant purpose" of gaining foreign intelligence information, the Patriot Act allows the government to have a primary objective of prosecuting an agent for a non-foreign intelligence crime. Yet we think that would be an anomalous reading of the amendment. For we see not the slightest indication that Congress meant to give that power to the Executive Branch. Accordingly, the manifestation of such a purpose, it seems to us, would continue to disqualify an application. That is not to deny that ordinary crimes might be inextricably intertwined with foreign intelligence crimes. For example, if a group of international terrorists were to engage in bank robberies in order to finance the manufacture of a bomb, evidence of the bank robbery should be treated just as evidence of the terrorist act itself. But the FISA process cannot be used as a device to investigate wholly unrelated ordinary crimes.

One final point; we think the government's purpose as set forth in a section 1804(a)(7)(B) certification is to be judged by the national security official's articulation and not by a FISA court inquiry into the origins of an investigation nor an examination of the personnel involved. It is up to the Director of the FBI, who typically certifies, to determine the government's national security purpose, as approved by the Attorney General or Deputy Attorney General. This is not a standard whose application the FISA court legitimately reviews by seeking to inquire into which Justice Department officials were instigators of an investigation. . . .

III.

Having determined that FISA, as amended, does not oblige the government to demonstrate to the FISA court that its primary purpose in conducting electronic surveillance is not criminal prosecution, we are obliged to consider whether the statute as amended is consistent with the Fourth Amendment. . . . The FISA court indicated that its disapproval of the Attorney General's 2002 Procedures was based on the need to safeguard the "privacy of Americans in these highly intrusive surveillances and searches," which implies the invocation of the Fourth Amendment. The government, recognizing the Fourth Amendment's shadow effect on the FISA court's

Chapter 12. Investigating Terrorism   35

opinion, has affirmatively argued that FISA is constitutional....

The FISA court expressed concern that unless FISA were "construed" in the fashion that it did, the government could use a FISA order as an improper substitute for an ordinary criminal warrant under Title III. That concern seems to suggest that the FISA court thought Title III procedures are constitutionally mandated if the government has a prosecutorial objective regarding an agent of a foreign power. But in United States v. United States District Court (*Keith*), 407 U.S. 297, 322 (1972) – in which the Supreme Court explicitly declined to consider foreign intelligence surveillance – the Court indicated that, even with respect to domestic national security intelligence gathering for prosecutorial purposes where a warrant was mandated, Title III procedures were not constitutionally required: "[W]e do not hold that the same type of standards and procedures prescribed by Title III are necessarily applicable to this case. We recognize that domestic security surveillance may involve different policy and practical considerations from the surveillance of 'ordinary crime.'" Nevertheless, in asking whether FISA procedures can be regarded as reasonable under the Fourth Amendment, we think it is instructive to compare those procedures and requirements with their Title III counterparts. Obviously, the closer those FISA procedures are to Title III procedures, the lesser are our constitutional concerns.

Comparison of FISA Procedures with Title III

... [W]hile Title III contains some protections that are not in FISA, in many significant respects the two statutes are equivalent, and in some, FISA contains additional protections. Still, to the extent the two statutes diverge in constitutionally relevant areas – in particular, in their probable cause and particularity showings – a FISA order may not be a "warrant" contemplated by the Fourth Amendment.... We do not decide the issue but note that to the extent a FISA order comes close to meeting Title III, that certainly bears on its reasonableness under the Fourth Amendment.

Did Truong Articulate the Appropriate Constitutional Standard?

Ultimately, the question becomes whether FISA, as amended by the Patriot Act, is a reasonable response based on a balance of the legitimate need of the government for foreign intelligence information to protect against national security threats with the protected rights of citizens....

It will be recalled that the case that set forth the primary purpose test *as constitutionally required* was *Truong*. The Fourth Circuit thought that

Keith's balancing standard implied the adoption of the primary purpose test. We reiterate that *Truong* dealt with a pre-FISA surveillance based on the President's constitutional responsibility to conduct the foreign affairs of the United States. 629 F.2d at 914. Although *Truong* suggested the line it drew was a constitutional minimum that would apply to a FISA surveillance, *see id.* at 914 n.4, it had no occasion to consider the application of the statute carefully. The *Truong* court, as did all the other courts to have decided the issue, held that the President did have inherent authority to conduct warrantless searches to obtain foreign intelligence information. It was incumbent upon the court, therefore, to determine the boundaries of that constitutional authority in the case before it. We take for granted that the President does have that authority and, assuming that is so, FISA could not encroach on the President's constitutional power. The question before us is the reverse, does FISA amplify the President's power by providing a mechanism that at least approaches a classic warrant and which therefore supports the government's contention that FISA searches are constitutionally reasonable.

The district court in the *Truong* case had excluded evidence obtained from electronic surveillance after the government's investigation – the court found – had converted from one conducted for foreign intelligence reasons to one conducted primarily as a criminal investigation. . . . The court of appeals endorsed that approach, stating:

> We think that the district court adopted the proper test, because once surveillance becomes primarily a criminal investigation, the courts are entirely competent to make the usual probable cause determination, and because, importantly, individual privacy interests come to the fore *and government foreign policy concerns recede* when the government is primarily attempting to form the basis of a criminal prosecution.

Id. at 915 (emphasis added).

That analysis, in our view, rested on a false premise and the line the court sought to draw was inherently unstable, unrealistic, and confusing. The false premise was the assertion that once the government moves to criminal prosecution, its "foreign policy concerns" recede. As we have discussed in the first part of the opinion, that is simply not true as it relates to counterintelligence. In that field the government's primary purpose is to halt the espionage or terrorism efforts, and criminal prosecutions can be, and usually are, interrelated with other techniques used to frustrate a foreign power's efforts. . . .

Recent testimony before the Joint Intelligence Committee amply demonstrates that the *Truong* line is a very difficult one to administer.

Chapter 12. Investigating Terrorism

Indeed, it was suggested that the FISA court requirements based on *Truong* may well have contributed, whether correctly understood or not, to the FBI missing opportunities to anticipate the September 11, 2001 attacks. That is not to say that we should be prepared to jettison Fourth Amendment requirements in the interest of national security. Rather, assuming *arguendo* that FISA orders are not Fourth Amendment warrants, the question becomes, are the searches constitutionally reasonable. And in judging reasonableness, the instability of the *Truong* line is a relevant consideration. . . .

Supreme Court's Special Needs Cases

The distinction between ordinary criminal prosecutions and extraordinary situations underlies the Supreme Court's approval of entirely warrantless and even suspicionless searches that are designed to serve the government's "special needs, beyond the normal need for law enforcement." Vernonia School Dist. 47J v. Acton, 515 U.S. 646, 653 (1995) (quoting Griffin v. Wisconsin, 483 U.S. 868, 873 (1987) (internal quotation marks omitted)) (random drug-testing of student athletes). Apprehending drunk drivers and securing the border constitute such unique interests beyond ordinary, general law enforcement. *Id.* at 654 (citing Michigan Dep't of State Police v. Sitz, 496 U.S. 444 (1990), and United States v. Martinez-Fuerte, 428 U.S. 543 (1976)). . . .

. . . The nature of the "emergency," which is simply another word for threat, takes the matter out of the realm of ordinary crime control.

Conclusion

FISA's general programmatic purpose, to protect the nation against terrorists and espionage threats directed by foreign powers, has from its outset been distinguishable from "ordinary crime control." After the events of September 11, 2001, though, it is hard to imagine greater emergencies facing Americans than those experienced on that date.

We acknowledge, however, that the constitutional question presented by this case – whether Congress's disapproval of the primary purpose test is consistent with the Fourth Amendment – has no definitive jurisprudential answer. The Supreme Court's special needs cases involve random stops (seizures) not electronic searches. In one sense, they can be thought of as a greater encroachment into personal privacy because they are not based on any particular suspicion. On the other hand, wiretapping is a good deal more intrusive than an automobile stop accompanied by questioning.

... Our case may well involve the most serious threat our country faces. Even without taking into account the President's inherent constitutional authority to conduct warrantless foreign intelligence surveillance, we think the procedures and government showings required under FISA, if they do not meet the minimum Fourth Amendment warrant standards, certainly come close. We, therefore, believe firmly, applying the balancing test drawn from *Keith*, that FISA as amended is constitutional because the surveillances it authorizes are reasonable.

Accordingly, we reverse the FISA court's orders in this case to the extent they imposed conditions on the grant of the government's applications, vacate the FISA court's Rule 11, and remand with instructions to grant the applications as submitted and proceed henceforth in accordance with this opinion.

NOTES AND QUESTIONS

1. *Defending the FISC (and the Public?) on Appeal.* No target of a FISC surveillance order ever learns about the issuance of the order, unless the information collected is later used in a criminal prosecution, as in *Duggan,* or turns up in a FOIA or Privacy Act request (see casebook Chapter 15). As a practical matter, therefore, there was no one who had a legally protected interest to process an appeal of the *FISCR* decision to the Supreme Court – or at least no one who knew she had such an interest. Nonetheless, public interest groups led by the ACLU filed a petition for leave to intervene and a petition for certiorari in the Supreme Court. Can you outline their likely positions, both on their right to intervene and on the merits? On March 24, 2003, the Supreme Court dismissed the petition. American Civil Liberties Union v. United States, 123 S. Ct. 1615 (2003) (Mem.). *See* Linda Greenhouse, *Opponents Lose Challenge to Government's Broader Use of Wiretaps to Fight Terrorism*, N.Y. Times, Mar. 25, 2003, at A12.

2. *The Holding.* What is the holding of the *FISCR* decision? Is the holding based on FISA, on the Constitution, or both? Can you reconcile the holding in the *FISCR* decision with *Keith*? With *Truong*?

3. *Purpose vs. Use.* If it has been the case since 1978 that foreign intelligence information includes evidence of foreign intelligence crimes, does this frequent overlap in the nature of the information bear upon the objective of the planned surveillance? Are the FISA limits concerned with the objective of the surveillance or the nature and subsequent uses of the

Chapter 12. Investigating Terrorism 39

information to be obtained?

The *FISC* decision emphasized the importance of preserving the foreign intelligence objectives of FISA. In view of those objectives, on what basis did the FISCR object to forbidding the Criminal Division from directing or controlling the use of FISA procedures? Is the alleged flaw in the FISC order based on the PATRIOT Act amendments to FISA, or would the infirmity have been present even if FISA had not been amended?

Can you now describe the significance of the PATRIOT Act amendment to the "purpose" requirement? Did the information-sharing additions to FISA in the PATRIOT Act contribute to the result? If so, how? Should Congress revisit the "purpose" standard in FISA? If so, should Congress codify the "primary purpose" requirement, or should it more clearly abandon any required foreign intelligence objectives in shaping requests to the FISC?

4. *The Minimization Requirements.* Why was the FISC in error for relying on the minimization requirements in FISA to justify its order? Do the minimization procedures imply a "wall" between the law enforcement and intelligence investigators?

5. *The "Special Needs" Precedents.* Are you persuaded that the Supreme Court's "special needs" cases are based on considerations that are analogous to the Justice Department procedures at issue in this appeal?

6. *The Aftermath.* Approximately six months after the *FISCR* decision, Justice Department officials reported to the House Judiciary Committee that the procedures approved by the FISCR have "allowed the Department of Justice to investigate cases in a more orderly, efficient, and knowledgeable way, and ha[ve] permitted all involved personnel, both law enforcement and intelligence, to discuss openly legal, factual, and tactical issues arising during the course of investigations. . . . The Department has developed counterterrorism tools and methods that plainly would not have been possible under the previous standards." Brown (p. 23 *supra*), at 15-16. The Department also reported that approximately 4,500 open intelligence files were shared with criminal prosecutors since October 2002 to allow the law enforcement personnel to determine whether criminal investigations should be initiated concerning any of those intelligence targets. *Id.*

D. EXECUTIVE AUTHORITY FOR NATIONAL SECURITY INVESTIGATIONS

1. Initiating Investigation

Page 700. Insert this material before the Attorney General's Domestic Security Guidelines.

On May 30, 2002, the FBI issued three new sets of guidelines for investigations that significantly revise the 1983 *Attorney General's Domestic Security Guidelines* set out in this section. They are the *Attorney General's Guidelines on General Crimes, Racketeering Enterprise and Terrorism Enterprise Investigations,* the *Attorney General's Guidelines on the Use of Confidential Informants,* and the *Attorney General's Guidelines on Federal Bureau of Investigation Undercover Operations,* available at http://www.usdoj.gov/olp/index.html#agguide. The *Attorney General Foreign Counterintelligence (FCI) Guidelines,* however, were not changed.

Two revisions are especially important for our purposes, one dealing with preliminary inquiries and the other with what are now called "terrorism enterprise investigations." Replacement sections are set out below and are followed by notes addressing these and other changes.

Page 702. Replace Domestic Security Guidelines §II.B.(4) and (5) with the following:

(4) The choice of investigative techniques in an inquiry is a matter of judgment, which should take account of: (i) the objectives of the inquiry and available investigative resources, (ii) the intrusiveness of a technique, considering such factors as the effect on the privacy of individuals and potential damage to reputation, (iii) the seriousness of the possible crime, and (iv) the strength of the information indicating its existence or future commission. Where the conduct of an inquiry presents a choice between the use of more or less intrusive methods, the FBI should consider whether the information could be obtained in a timely and effective way by the less intrusive means. The FBI should not hesitate to use any lawful techniques consistent with these Guidelines in an inquiry, even if intrusive, where the intrusiveness is warranted in light of the seriousness of the possible crime or the strength of the information indicating its existence or future commission. This point is to be particularly observed in inquiries relating to possible terrorist activities.

Chapter 12. Investigating Terrorism 41

(5) All lawful investigative techniques may be used in an inquiry except:

(a) Mail openings; and

(b) Nonconsensual electronic surveillance or any other investigative technique covered by chapter 119 of title 18, United States Code (18 U.S.C. 2510-2522).

Pages 703-704. Replace Domestic Security Guidelines §§III.B.1 thru 4 with the following:

1. General Authority

a. A terrorism enterprise investigation may be initiated when facts or circumstances reasonably indicate that two or more persons are engaged in an enterprise for the purpose of: (i) furthering political or social goals wholly or in part through activities that involve force or violence and a violation of federal criminal law, (ii) engaging in terrorism as defined in 18 U.S.C. 2331(1) or (5) that involves a violation of federal criminal law, or (iii) committing any offense described in 18 U.S.C. 2332b(g)(5)(B). A terrorism enterprise investigation may also be initiated when facts or circumstances reasonably indicate that two or more persons are engaged in a pattern of racketeering activity as defined in the RICO statute, 18 U.S.C. 1961(5), that involves an offense or offenses described in 18 U.S.C. 2332b(g)(5)(B). The standard of "reasonable indication" is identical to that governing the initiation of a general crimes investigation under Part II. In determining whether an investigation should be conducted, the FBI shall consider all of the circumstances including: (i) the magnitude of the threatened harm; (ii) the likelihood it will occur; (iii) the immediacy of the threat; and (iv) any danger to privacy or free expression posed by an investigation. . . .

c. Mere speculation that force or violence might occur during the course of an otherwise peaceable demonstration is not sufficient grounds for initiation of an investigation under this Subpart, but where facts or circumstances reasonably indicate that a group or enterprise has engaged or aims to engage in activities involving force or violence or other criminal conduct described in paragraph (1)(a) in a demonstration, an investigation may be initiated in conformity with the standards of that paragraph. . . . This does not limit the collection of information about public demonstrations by enterprises that are under active investigation pursuant to paragraph (1)(a) above. . . .

4. *Authorization and Renewal*

a. A terrorism enterprise investigation may be authorized by the Special Agent in Charge, with notification to FBIHQ, upon a written recommendation setting forth the facts or circumstances reasonably indicating the existence of an enterprise as described in paragraph (1)(a)....

Page 706. Add this material at the end of Note 7.

The Introduction to the *2002 Domestic Security Guidelines* describes and explains the checking of leads and preliminary inquiries:

> The lowest level of investigative activity is the "prompt and extremely limited checking out of initial leads," which should be undertaken whenever information is received of such a nature that some follow-up as to the possibility of criminal activity is warranted. This limited activity should be conducted with an eye toward promptly determining whether further investigation (either a preliminary inquiry or a full investigation) should be conducted.
>
> The next level of investigative activity, a preliminary inquiry, should be undertaken when there is information or an allegation which indicates the possibility of criminal activity and whose responsible handling requires some further scrutiny beyond checking initial leads. This authority allows FBI agents to respond to information that is ambiguous or incomplete. Even where the available information meets only this threshold, the range of available investigative techniques is broad....
>
> Whether it is appropriate to open a preliminary inquiry immediately, or instead to engage first in a limited checking out of leads, depends on the circumstances presented. If, for example, an agent receives an allegation that an individual or group has advocated the commission of criminal violence, and no other facts are available, an appropriate first step would be checking out of leads to determine whether the individual, group, or members of the audience have the apparent ability or intent to carry out the advocated crime. A similar response would be appropriate on the basis of non-verbal conduct of an ambiguous character – for example, where a report is received that an individual has accumulated explosives that could be used either in a legitimate business or to commit a terrorist act. Where the limited checking out of leads discloses a possibility or reasonable indication of criminal activity, a preliminary inquiry or full investigation may then be initiated. However, if the available information shows at the outset that the threshold standard for a preliminary inquiry or full investigation is satisfied, then the appropriate investigative activity may be initiated immediately, without progressing through more limited investigative stages.

Chapter 12. Investigating Terrorism 43

> The application of these Guidelines' standards for inquiries merits special attention in cases that involve efforts by individuals or groups to obtain, for no apparent reason, biological, chemical, radiological, or nuclear materials whose use or possession is constrained by such statutes as 18 U.S.C. 175, 229, or 831. For example, FBI agents are not required to possess information relating to an individual's intended criminal use of dangerous biological agents or toxins prior to initiating investigative activity. On the contrary, if an individual or group has attempted to obtain such materials, or has indicated a desire to acquire them, and the reason is not apparent, investigative action, such as conducting a checking out of leads or initiating a preliminary inquiry, may be appropriate to determine whether there is a legitimate purpose for the possession of the materials by the individual or group. Likewise, where individuals or groups engage in efforts to acquire or show an interest in acquiring, without apparent reason, toxic chemicals or their precursors or radiological or nuclear materials, investigative action to determine whether there is a legitimate purpose may be justified.

What changes from the 1983 preliminary inquiry rules are reflected in the new statement? Are you satisfied that the changes are merited? That they are lawful?

Page 707. Add this material at the end of Note 8.

The 2002 guidelines add that a full investigation "may be conducted to prevent, solve, or prosecute" criminal activity. *2002 Domestic Security Guidelines* §II.C.1. Otherwise, the new Terrorism Enterprise Investigations category (replacing Domestic Security/Terrorism Investigations in Part II.B of the 1983 guidelines) supplies new authority for FBI full investigations. Does the "reasonable indication" standard continue to provide an adequate benchmark for preserving privacy or First Amendment interests?

Page 707. Add this material at the end of Note 9.

Why do you suppose the Attorney General revised the Domestic Security Guidelines in the wake of the September 11 terrorist attacks but not the FCI Guidelines?

2. Choosing and Regulating the Means of Investigation

Page 711. Add this material at the end of Note 2.

The 2002 guidelines change the "undisclosed participation" strictures, providing instead that any such investigation that could raise "potential constitutional concerns relating to activities of the organization protected by the First Amendment" must comply with the *Attorney General's Guidelines on FBI Undercover Operations* and the *Attorney General's Guidelines Regarding the Use of Informants. 2002 Domestic Security Guidelines* §IV.B.3.

An undercover operation uses a government employee whose relationship with the FBI is concealed from third parties in the course of an investigation, *Undercover Operations Guidelines, supra,* §§II.B, C, while a confidential informant is any person who provides useful and credible information. *Confidential Informants Guidelines* §I.B.6. The *Confidential Informants Guidelines* do not mention the First Amendment interests of groups that may be infiltrated by an informant or undercover agent, and the *Undercover Operations Guidelines* simply say that any official empowered to authorize an undercover operation should give "careful consideration" to the "risk of invasion of privacy or interference with privileged or confidential relationships and any potential constitutional concerns or other legal concerns" in deciding whether to approve an application. *Undercover Operations Guidelines* §IV.A.(3). Do you think that these provisions are constitutional?

The different predicate standards for using informants in the two levels of investigation are due to a broader range of investigative techniques permitted in a full investigation. Do you think the differences between inquiry and full investigations have narrowed in this respect after the 2002 revisions?

Page 712. Add this material at the end of Note 5.

The 2002 *Domestic Security Guidelines* removed mail covers from the list of forbidden techniques during preliminary inquiries. §II.B.5. They also added potentially important and constitutionally controversial new authority for FBI investigations in counterterrorism, in reaction to September 11 and the continuing threat of terrorism. Three broad investigative activities are authorized: (1) surfing the Internet to identify Web sites, bulletin boards, chat rooms, and the like where terrorist or other criminal activities might be detected; (2) attending public events and

Chapter 12. Investigating Terrorism 45

visiting public places for the purpose of detecting terrorist activity; and (3) using data-mining services to search for terrorists and terrorist activities. *See Domestic Security Guidelines* §§VI.A.1, 2; VI.B. According to DOJ officials, the decision to spell out the authorities in these three areas was based on the fact that the prior guidelines were widely regarded as exclusive; if something was not explicitly permitted, it was viewed as barred. *See New Rules Allow FBI Greater Use of Web, Visits to Public Places in Terrorism Probes*, 70 U.S.L.W. 2779 (June 11, 2002). What are the implications of the DOJ explanation for the scope and meaning of the new guidelines?

Some groups reacted by claiming that the new authorities would permit "fishing expeditions" and would chill protected expression in places like mosques, libraries, and Internet chat rooms, and at public gatherings in support of Palestinian or Islamic causes. *See* Center for Democracy & Technology, *CDT's Analysis of New FBI Guidelines*, May 30, 2002, *available at http://www.cdt.org/wiretap/020530guidelines.shtml*; Adam Liptak, *Changing the Standard: Despite Civil Liberties Fears, FBI Faces No Legal Obstacles on Domestic Spying*, N.Y. Times, May 31, 2002, A1.

Section VI.A of the 2002 *Domestic Security Guidelines* provides:

1. Information Systems

The FBI is authorized to operate and participate in identification, tracking, and information systems for the purpose of identifying and locating terrorists. . . . Systems within the scope of this paragraph may draw on and retain pertinent information from any source permitted by law, including information derived from past or ongoing investigative activities; other information collected or provided by governmental entities, such as foreign intelligence information and lookout list information; publicly available information, whether obtained directly or through services or resources (whether nonprofit or commercial) that compile or analyze such information; and information voluntarily provided by private entities. Any such system operated by the FBI shall be reviewed periodically for compliance with all applicable statutory provisions, Department regulations and policies, and Attorney General Guidelines.

2. Visiting Public Places and Events

For the purpose of detecting or preventing terrorist activities, the FBI is authorized to visit any place and attend any event that is open to the public, on the same terms and conditions as members of the public generally. No information obtained from such visits shall be retained unless it relates to potential or terrorist activity.

According to the Justice Department, under the previous guidelines "agents were reluctant to follow suspected terrorists into mosques." Brown (p. 23 *supra*), at 39. Was the agents' reluctance justified as a matter of law? Do the new guidelines solve whatever problem might have existed?

Section VI.B of the 2002 *Domestic Security Guidelines* authorizes the FBI to carry out "general topical research" online, defined as "concerning subject areas that are relevant for the purpose of facilitation or supporting the discharge of investigative responsibilities . . . [but] does not include online searches for information by individuals' names or other individual identifiers, except where such searches are incidental to topical research, such as searching to locate writings on a topic by searching under the names of authors who write on the topic, or searching by the name of a party to a case in conducting legal research." The introduction to Section VI states that the activities described may be carried out without regard to the predicates for the levels of investigative activity described in the guidelines.

Page 716. Add this material before the first full paragraph.

The Homeland Security Act further amended FISA by permitting intelligence officers to consult with state and local law enforcement officers regarding foreign intelligence information. Pub. L. No. 107-296, §898, 116 Stat. 2258 (2002), amending 50 U.S.C. §1806(k)(1).

E. PROFILING SUSPECTS FOR INVESTIGATION

Page 726. Add this material after the carryover paragraph.

On June 17, 2003, the Bush Administration issued guidelines barring federal agents from using race or ethnicity in investigations. However, the policy explicitly exempts national security and terrorism investigations and permits agents to use race and ethnicity in "narrow" circumstances. Eric Lichtblau, *Bush Issues Racial Profiling Ban But Exempts Security Inquiries*, N.Y. Times, June 18, 2003, at A1. The Justice Department offered examples of how the policy applies, including one which asserts that when officials learn that "terrorists from a particular ethnic group are planning to use commercial jetliners as weapons by hijacking them at an airport in California during the next week, . . . men of that ethnic group" boarding planes in California may be subjected to "heightened scrutiny." *Justice Department Guidance Regarding the Use of Race by Federal Law*

Chapter 12. Investigating Terrorism 47

Enforcement Agencies, www.usdoj.gov/crt/split/documents/guidance_on_race.htm. What is the legal effect of the new policy? Do you see any potential legal problems with implementing the policy in the California hijacking situation?

In a Justice Department report released earlier in June 2003, the DOJ Inspector General found that in the months after the September 11 attacks, many illegal immigrants with no connection to terrorism were detained under harsh conditions for lengthy periods. *See* Michael Moss, *False Terrorism Tips to FBI Uproot the Lives of Suspects*, N.Y. Times, June 19, 2003, at A1. The detention report is considered below. A New York Times investigation of court records and interviews also showed "that even seemingly plausible information from tipsters who eagerly came forward to identify themselves has led to misguided investigations." *Id*. Does the Bush administration's profiling policy respond effectively to the problem of relying on questionable sources to launch terrorism investigations? Can you outline a better policy?

F. PREVENTIVE DETENTION

Page 732. Add this material before Notes and Questions.

Office of the Inspector General, Department of Justice, Press Release, The September 11 Detainees: A Review of the Treatment of Aliens Held on Immigration Charges in Connection with the Investigation of the September 11 Attacks
June 2, 2003
http://www.usdoj.gov/oig/special/03-06/press.htm

After the September 11 terrorist attacks, the Department of Justice (Department) used federal immigration laws to detain aliens in the United States who were suspected of having ties to the attacks or connections to terrorism, or who were encountered during the course of the Federal Bureau of Investigation's (FBI) investigation into the attacks. In the 11 months after the attacks, 762 aliens were detained in connection with the FBI terrorism investigation for various immigration offenses, including overstaying their visas and entering the country illegally.

The Office of the Inspector General (OIG) examined the treatment of these detainees, including their processing, bond decisions related to them, the timing of their removal from the United States or their release from custody, their access to counsel, and their conditions of confinement. . . . Among the specific findings in the OIG's report:

Arrest, Charging & Assignment to a Detention Facility

• The FBI in New York City made little attempt to distinguish between aliens who were subjects of the FBI terrorism investigation (called "PENTTBOM") and those encountered coincidentally to a PENTTBOM lead. The OIG report concluded that, even in the chaotic aftermath of the September 11 attacks, the FBI should have expended more effort attempting to distinguish between aliens who it actually suspected of having a connection to terrorism from [sic] those aliens who, while possibly guilty of violating federal immigration law, had no connection to terrorism but simply were encountered in connection with a PENTTBOM lead.

• The INS did not consistently serve the September 11 detainees with notice of the charges under which they were being held within the INS's stated goal of 72 hours. The review found that some detainees did not receive these charging documents (called a "Notice to Appear"or NTA) for more than a month after being arrested. This delay affected the detainees' ability to understand why they were being held, obtain legal counsel, and request a bond hearing. . . .

• The Department instituted a policy that all aliens in whom the FBI had an interest in connection with the PENTTBOM investigation required clearance by the FBI of any connection to terrorism before they could be removed or released. Although not communicated in writing, this "hold until cleared" policy was clearly understood and applied throughout the Department. The policy was based on the belief – which turned out to be erroneous – that the FBI's clearance process would proceed quickly. FBI agents responsible for clearance investigations often were assigned other duties and were not able to focus on the detainee cases. The result was that detainees remained in custody – many in extremely restrictive conditions of confinement – for weeks and months with no clearance investigations being conducted. The OIG review found that, instead of taking a few days as anticipated, the FBI clearance process took an average of 80 days, primarily because it was understaffed and not given sufficient priority by the FBI.

Bond and Removal Issues

• The Department instituted a "no bond" policy for all September 11 detainees as part of its effort to keep the detainees confined until the FBI could complete its clearance investigations. The OIG review found that the INS raised concerns about this blanket "no bond" policy, particularly when it became clear that the FBI's clearance process was much slower than anticipated and the INS had little information in many individual

Chapter 12. Investigating Terrorism

cases on which to base its continued opposition to bond in immigration hearings. INS officials also were concerned about continuing to hold detainees while the FBI conducted clearance investigations where detainees had received a final removal or voluntary departure order. The OIG review found that the INS and the Department did not timely address conflicting interpretations of federal immigration law about detaining aliens with final orders of removal who wanted and were able to leave the country, but who had not been cleared by the FBI.

• In January 2002, when the FBI brought the issue of the extent of the INS's detention authority to the Department's attention, the Department abruptly changed its position as to whether the INS should continue to hold aliens after they had received a final departure or removal order until the FBI had completed the clearance process. After this time, the Department allowed the INS to remove aliens with final orders without FBI clearance. In addition, in many cases the INS failed to review the detainees' custody determination as required by federal regulations.

The FBI's initial assessment of the September 11 detainees' possible connections to terrorism and the slow pace of the clearance process had significant ramifications on the detainees' conditions of confinement. Our review found that 84 September 11 detainees were housed at the MDC [Metropolitan Detention Center] in Brooklyn under highly restrictive conditions. These conditions included "lock down" for at least 23 hours per day; escort procedures that included a "4-man hold" with handcuffs, leg irons, and heavy chains any time the detainees were moved outside their cells; and a limit of one legal telephone call per week and one social call per month.

Among the OIG review's findings regarding the treatment of detainees held at the MDC and Passaic are:

Conditions of Confinement

• BOP officials imposed a communications blackout for September 11 detainees immediately after the terrorist attacks that lasted several weeks. After the blackout period ended, the MDC's designation of the September 11 detainees as "Witness Security" inmates frustrated efforts by detainees' attorneys, families, and even law enforcement officials, to determine where the detainees were being held. We found that MDC staff frequently – and mistakenly – told people who inquired about a specific September 11 detainee that the detainee was not held at the facility when, in fact, the opposite was true.

• The MDC's restrictive and inconsistent policies on telephone access for detainees prevented some detainees from obtaining legal counsel in a timely manner. Most of the September 11 detainees did not have legal representation prior to their detention at the MDC. Consequently, the policy developed by the MDC that permitted detainees one legal call per week – while complying with broad BOP national standards – severely limited the detainees' ability to obtain and consult with legal counsel. In addition, we found that in many instances MDC staff did not ask detainees if they wanted their one legal call each week. We also found that the list of pro bono attorneys provided to the detainees contained inaccurate and outdated information.

- With regard to allegations of abuse at the MDC, the evidence indicates a pattern of physical and verbal abuse by some correctional officers at the MDC against some September 11 detainees, particularly during the first months after the attacks and during intake and movement of prisoners. Although the allegations of abuse have been declined for criminal prosecution, the OIG is continuing to investigate these matters administratively.

- The OIG review found that certain conditions of confinement at the MDC were unduly harsh, such as subjecting the September 11 detainees to having two lights illuminated in their cells 24 hours a day for several months longer than necessary, even after electricians rewired the cellblock to allow the lights to be turned off individually. We also found that MDC staff failed to inform MDC detainees in a timely manner about the process for filing formal complaints about their treatment.

- By contrast, the OIG review found that the detainees confined at Passaic had much different, and significantly less harsh, experiences than the MDC detainees. According to INS data, Passaic housed 400 September 11 detainees from the date of the terrorist attacks through May 30, 2002, the largest number of September 11 detainees held at any single U.S. detention facility. Passaic detainees housed in the general population were treated like "regular" INS detainees who also were held at the facility. Although we received some allegations of physical and verbal abuse, we did not find the evidence indicated a pattern of abuse at Passaic. However, the INS did not conduct sufficient and regular visits to Passaic to ensure the September 11 detainees' conditions of confinement were appropriate.

"The Justice Department faced enormous challenges as a result of the September 11 terrorist attacks, and its employees worked with dedication to meet these challenges," [Inspector General] Fine said. "The findings of our review should in no way diminish their work. However, while the chaotic situation and the uncertainties surrounding the detainees' connections to terrorism explain some of the problems we found in our review, they do not explain them all," Fine said. . . .

Chapter 12. Investigating Terrorism 51

Page 732. Add this material at the end of Note 1.

In Denmore v. Hyung Joon Kim, 123 S. Ct. 1708 (2003), Justice Souter summarized the due process requirements for preventive detention as follows:

> [D]ue process requires a "special justification" for physical detention that "outweighs the individual's constitutionally protected interest in avoiding physical restraint" as well as "adequate procedural protections." "There must be a 'sufficiently compelling' governmental interest to justify such an action, usually a punitive interest in imprisoning the convicted criminal or a regulatory interest in forestalling danger to the community." The class of persons subject to confinement must be commensurately narrow and the duration of confinement limited accordingly. . . . Finally, procedural due process requires, at a minimum, that a detainee have the benefit of an impartial decisionmaker able to consider particular circumstances on the issue of necessity.

Id. at 1736 (Souter, J., concurring in part and dissenting in part).

Applying such standards, in United States v. Salerno, 481 U.S. 739 (1987), a divided Supreme Court upheld the provisions of the Bail Reform Act of 1984, 18 U.S.C. §3142(e), which authorized preventive detention (denial of bail) of arrestees on the grounds of flight risk or future dangerousness. The majority found that the Act authorized a "regulatory," rather than punitive, detention that was reasonably related to compelling government interests. The Court noted that regulatory interests in community safety can outweigh an individual's liberty interest, "[f]or example, in times of war and insurrection." 481 U.S. at 748. But it emphasized that the Bail Reform Act authorized detention of an arrestee only when: (a) he has been arrested and indicted on probable cause of having committed one or more specified extremely dangerous offenses, (b) a court conducts a full-blown adversary hearing on denial of bail at which the arrestee is entitled to be represented by his own counsel, (c) the government persuades the court by clear and convincing evidence that no conditions of release can assure the presence of the arrestee or the safety of the community, and (d) the arrestee is given a right of appeal from the court's decision.

Do the post-September 11 detentions described above satisfy the due process standards? Even if they do, does the Bail Reform Act occupy the field of preventive detention (leaving aside immigration detentions)? See additional material in this Supplement for p. 734, Note 4 *infra*.

Page 734. Add this material at the end of Note 3.

At the end of 2002, at least 44 persons were reported to have been detained as material witnesses in the September 11 investigation. Steve Fainaru & Margot Williams, *Material Witness Law Has Many in Limbo*, Wash. Post, Nov. 24, 2002, at A1. Half of them were held for more than 60 days. Brown (p. 23 *supra*), at 50.

The district courts have disagreed about the legality of these detentions. Emphasizing that the material witness statute contemplates testimony of a material witness "in a criminal proceeding," 18 U.S.C. §3144, one court asserted that interpreting the statute to allow imprisonment of a material witness for a grand jury investigation (as opposed to pending criminal trial) would pose serious Fourth Amendment questions. United States v. Awadallah, 202 F. Supp. 2d 55 (S.D.N.Y. 2002). "[S]ince 1789, no Congress has granted the government the authority to imprison an innocent person in order to guarantee that he will testify before a grand jury," it added, and therefore found such detention to be unlawful. *Id.* at 82. In contrast, in In re Application of the United States for a Material Witness Warrant, 213 F. Supp. 2d 287 (S.D.N.Y. 2002), the court held that "criminal proceeding" in the material witness statute included a grand jury investigation. It then found that imprisoning even an innocent man to obtain his evidence in a criminal proceeding is constitutional because "[t]he public has a right to everyman's evidence," *id.* at 298, quoting United States v. Burr, 25 Fed. Cas. 38 (No. 14,962e) (C.C. Va. 1807) (Marshall, C.J.).

Does it make any practical difference whether the "criminal proceeding" is a pending criminal trial or a grand jury? Consider how your answer might bear on whether the witness is material or on how long the witness can be detained.

Page 734. Add this material at the end of Note 4.

As the OIG report suggests, immigration laws, like the Bail Reform Act (see *supra*), authorize immigration judges to deny bond for a detained immigrant if the government provides evidence of flight risk or dangerousness. The FBI, however, provided no information to sustain such determinations in many cases. Nevertheless, INS lawyers were apparently ordered to argue the "no bond" position in court without any evidence, using "boilerplate" affidavits like the Rolince affidavit set out in the casebook at p. 729. *See* U.S. Department of Justice, Office of the Inspector General, *The September 11 Detainees: A Review of the Treatment of Aliens Held on Immigration Charges in Connection With the Investigation of the September 11 Attacks* 78-80 (June 2003). Was this ethical? *Id.* at 79, 81.

Chapter 12. Investigating Terrorism 53

In some cases, the alien succeeded in obtaining a bond order and posting bond, but the INS, without appealing the order, continued to hold him anyway. Was this lawful? *Id.* at 87 (reporting that one INS official admitted not knowing what to tell the immigrant's lawyer, "because I cannot bring myself to say that the INS no longer feels compelled to obey the law"). How far may a government lawyer go in defending preventive detention if he is instructed that it is essential to a terrorism investigation?

In Denmore v. Hyung Joon Kim, 123 S. Ct. 1708 (2003), the Supreme Court revisited the issue of immigration detention, this time considering a statutory provision for mandatory detention of criminal aliens pending their removal hearings. Admitting that individualized bond hearings might be feasible, the majority nevertheless concluded that "when the Government deals with deportable aliens, the Due Process Clause does not require it to employ the least burdensome means to accomplish its goal." *Id.* at 1720. It therefore upheld the mandatory detention law, but emphasized that such detentions pending removal were for less than ninety days in the majority of cases. Joining in the opinion, Justice Kennedy noted that if the removal proceedings were unreasonably delayed, "it could become necessary then to inquire whether the detention is not to facilitate deportation, or to protect against risk of flight or dangerousness, but to incarcerate for other reasons." *Id.* at 1722 (Kennedy, J., concurring). How would the post-September 11 immigration detentions described in the OIG report fare by these standards?

Page 735. Add this material at the end of Note 6.

At the same time that it repealed the Emergency Detention Act, Congress adopted a new measure stating, "No citizen shall be imprisoned or otherwise detained by the United States except pursuant to an Act of Congress." 18 U.S.C. §4001(a). Does this provision apply to the detention of suspected terrorists? Application of the new provision was considered in two recent cases, set out at pp. 57 and 69 in this Supplement.

Page 736. Add this material at the end of Note 7.

Which, if any, of the foregoing rights were violated during the post-September 11 detention of immigrants described in the OIG report? Shortly after publication of the report, a divided panel of the D.C. Circuit Court of Appeals found that various public interest groups had no right under the Freedom of Information Act or First Amendment to assorted details of the post-September 11 detentions, which they sought in part to ascertain the legality of the detention and conditions of confinement. Center for National

Security Studies v. United States Dept. of Justice, 331 F.3d 918 (D.C. Cir. 2003), reproduced in this Supplement at p. 101. Based presumably on the government's representations, a majority of the panel assumed that the immigrant detainees "have had access to counsel, and the INS has provided detainees with lists of attorneys willing to represent them. . . . They have also been free to disclose their names to the public." *Id.* In light of the OIG report, were these assumptions warranted?

13

Consequence Management: When the Worst Happens

B. WHO'S IN CHARGE? TAKING COMMAND OF THE SITUATION

2. Addressing Medical Emergencies

c. *Civil Liberties Implications*

Page 764. Add the following materials after Note 3.

4. *SARS and the Locus of Authority.* The Sudden Acute Respiratory Syndrome (SARS) epidemic that mysteriously appeared in the spring of 2003 caused public health officials to revisit the prospect of quarantine as a public health measure. On April 1, when seven passengers on an American Airlines flight from Tokyo to San Jose, California, experienced flu-like symptoms, Santa Clara County health officials surrounded the aircraft with emergency vehicles after it landed. The passengers were given a choice – go with county officials for examination and potential quarantine, or go home and about their business, at the risk of spreading SARS. Five went with the county teams, two went home, and none developed SARS. Santa Clara County officials then complained that they lacked authority to order detention or confinement of possible SARS patients. Melissa Healy, *Are Quarantines Back?*, L.A. Times, Apr. 14, 2003. Was their concern well-founded? On April 4, President Bush added SARS to the list of diseases for which federal officials may quarantine citizens. Exec. Order No. 13,295, 68 Fed. Reg. 17,255 (2003). Does the new order provide adequate authority for public health officials to respond to the threat of SARS? Should Santa Clara County take additional measures? If so, which ones?

55

5. *Smallpox Vaccination Plan Update.* The federal campaign to vaccinate 500,000 health care workers against smallpox stalled in the first months of 2003 when only about 35,000 workers agreed to be inoculated. Because adequate numbers of volunteers did not come forward, public health officials revised smallpox preparedness plans to acknowledge the likely need to vaccinate doctors and nurses after, rather than before, an outbreak begins. Christian Davenport, *Smallpox Strategies Shifting: Inoculations Fall Far Short of Goals of Nation, Region*, Wash. Post, May 12, 2003, at A1. More than 450,000 military personnel were also vaccinated by June 2003. Both the civilian and military programs were "paused" in June 2003; the military program was halted because it had already inoculated everyone who was eligible. Donald G. McNeil, Jr., *2 Programs to Vaccinate for Smallpox Are "Paused,"* N.Y. Times, June 19, 2003, at A13.

C. SPECIAL THREATS TO CIVIL LIBERTIES IN A CRISIS

Page 810. Add this material after Note 13.

1.1. Military Detention

The military detention of Japanese-Americans during World War II was unusual for its location – inside the United States – and its targets – non-combatant U.S. citizens. But in war, the military has frequently and uncontroversially taken prisoners and detained combatants as part of a military operation or to protect its forces in the field. Does it have such wartime detention authority during a "war on terrorism"? Can any such authority operate within the United States or elsewhere away from the battlefield? Does it extend to citizen combatants? Besides *Korematsu*, the most important historical Supreme Court precedents are Ex parte Milligan, 71 U.S. (4 Wall.) 2 (1866), and Ex parte Quirin, 317 U.S. 1 (1942). Both cases expressly addressed the legality only of *trial by military commission* (treated in some detail at casebook pp. 889-906), but they are impliedly relevant also to *detention,* insofar as military trial of a combatant necessarily presupposes military detention of him as well.

Chapter 13. Consequence Management: When the Worst Happens   57

Ex parte Milligan
United States Supreme Court, 1866
71 U.S. (4 Wall.) 2

[Parts of the opinion are set forth at casebook pp. 786 and 889.]

Ex parte Quirin
United States Supreme Court, 1942
317 U.S. 1

[The opinion is set forth at casebook p. 893.]

NOTES AND QUESTIONS

[See Notes 1-5, casebook pp. 901-904.]

After 9/11, the government placed several alleged "enemy combatants" in military detention, citing *Quirin* as authority, in part. We consider next the case of Yaser Hamdi, an American citizen, who was allegedly captured on the battlefield in Afghanistan. We then turn to the military detention of José Padilla, another U.S. citizen. Padilla was captured not on the battlefield, but in Chicago. The President designated him an enemy combatant as a basis for his transfer from civilian to military custody.

Hamdi v. Rumsfeld
United States Court of Appeals, 4th Circuit, 2003
316 F.3d 450, *reh'g denied en banc,* 2003 WL 21540768

WILKINSON, Chief Judge, and WILKINS and TRAXLER, Circuit Judges. Yaser Esam Hamdi filed a petition under 28 U.S.C. §2241 challenging the lawfulness of his confinement in the Norfolk Naval Brig. On this third and latest appeal, the United States challenges the district court's order requiring the production of various materials regarding Hamdi's status as an alleged enemy combatant. The district court certified for appeal the question of whether a declaration by a Special Advisor to the Under Secretary of Defense for Policy setting forth what the government contends were the circumstances of Hamdi's capture was sufficient by itself to justify his detention. Because it is undisputed that Hamdi was captured in a zone of active combat in a foreign theater of conflict, we hold that the submitted declaration is a sufficient basis upon which to conclude that the Commander in Chief has constitutionally detained Hamdi pursuant to the war powers entrusted to him by the United States Constitution. No further factual inquiry is necessary or proper, and we remand the case with directions to dismiss the petition.

I. . . .

The present case arises out of Hamdi's detention by the United States military in Norfolk, Virginia. Hamdi apparently was born in Louisiana but left for Saudi Arabia when he was a small child. . . .

In June 2002, Hamdi's father, Esam Fouad Hamdi, filed a petition for writ of habeas corpus, naming as petitioners both Hamdi and himself as next friend. The petition alleged that Hamdi is a citizen of the United States who was residing in Afghanistan when he was seized by the United States government. . . .

On July 25, the government filed a response to, and motion to dismiss, the petition for a writ of habeas corpus. Attached to its response was an affidavit from the Special Advisor to the Under Secretary of Defense for Policy, Michael Mobbs, which confirms the material factual allegations in Hamdi's petition – specifically, that Hamdi was seized in Afghanistan by allied military forces during the course of the sanctioned military campaign, designated an "enemy combatant" by our Government, and ultimately transferred to the Norfolk Naval Brig for detention. . . .

In addition to stating that Hamdi has been classified as an enemy combatant, the Mobbs declaration went on further to describe what the government contends were the circumstances surrounding Hamdi's seizure, his transfer to United States custody, and his placement in the Norfolk Naval Brig. According to Mobbs, the military determined that Hamdi "traveled to Afghanistan in approximately July or August of 2001" and proceeded to "affiliate[ ] with a Taliban military unit and receive[ ] weapons training." While serving with the Taliban in the wake of September 11, he was captured when his Taliban unit surrendered to Northern Alliance forces with which it had been engaged in battle. He was in possession of an AK-47 rifle at the time of surrender. Hamdi was then transported with his unit from Konduz, Afghanistan to the Northern Alliance prison in Mazar-e-Sharif, Afghanistan and, after a prison uprising there, to a prison at Sheberghan, Afghanistan. Hamdi was next transported to the U.S. short term detention facility in Kandahar, and then transferred again to Guantanamo Bay and eventually to the Norfolk Naval Brig. According to Mobbs, interviews with Hamdi confirmed the details of his capture and his status as an enemy combatant. . . .

Chapter 13. Consequence Management: When the Worst Happens

The district court filed an opinion on August 16, finding that the Mobbs declaration "falls far short" of supporting Hamdi's detention. The court ordered the government to turn over, among other things, copies of Hamdi's statements and the notes taken from any interviews with him; the names and addresses of all interrogators who have questioned Hamdi; statements by members of the Northern Alliance regarding the circumstances of Hamdi's surrender; and a list of the date of Hamdi's capture and all of the dates and locations of his subsequent detention. . . .

II.

Yaser Esam Hamdi is apparently an American citizen. He was also captured by allied forces in Afghanistan, a zone of active military operations. This dual status – that of American citizen and that of alleged enemy combatant – raises important questions about the role of the courts in times of war.

A.

The importance of limitations on judicial activities during wartime may be inferred from the allocation of powers under our constitutional scheme. "Congress and the President, like the courts, possess no power not derived from the Constitution." Ex parte Quirin, 317 U.S. 1, 25 (1942). . . .

The war powers thus invest "the President, as Commander in Chief, with the power to wage war which Congress has declared, and to carry into effect all laws passed by Congress for the conduct of war and for the government and regulation of the Armed Forces, and all laws defining and punishing offences against the law of nations, including those which pertain to the conduct of war." *Quirin,* 317 U.S. at 26. These powers include the authority to detain those captured in armed struggle. [Hamdi v. Rumsfeld, 296 F.3d 278 (4th Cir. 2002) (*Hamdi II*),] at 281-82.[3] These powers likewise extend to the executive's decision to deport or detain alien enemies during the duration of hostilities, *see* Ludecke v. Watkins, 335 U.S. 160, 173 (1948) . . . .

Article III contains nothing analogous to the specific powers of war so carefully enumerated in Articles I and II. "In accordance with this

---

3. Persons captured during wartime are often referred to as "enemy combatants." While the designation of Hamdi as an "enemy combatant" has aroused controversy, the term is one that has been used by the Supreme Court many times. *See, e.g.,* Madsen v. Kinsella, 343 U.S. 341, 355 (1952); In re Yamashita, 327 U.S. 1, 7 (1946); *Quirin,* 317 U.S. at 31.

constitutional text, the Supreme Court has shown great deference to the political branches when called upon to decide cases implicating sensitive matters of foreign policy, national security, or military affairs." *Hamdi II,* 296 F.3d at 281.

The reasons for this deference are not difficult to discern. Through their departments and committees, the executive and legislative branches are organized to supervise the conduct of overseas conflict in a way that the judiciary simply is not. The Constitution's allocation of the warmaking powers reflects not only the expertise and experience lodged within the executive, but also the more fundamental truth that those branches most accountable to the people should be the ones to undertake the ultimate protection and to ask the ultimate sacrifice from them. Thus the Supreme Court has lauded "[t]he operation of a healthy deference to legislative and executive judgments in the area of military affairs." Rostker v. Goldberg, 453 U.S. 57, 66 (1981).

The deference that flows from the explicit enumeration of powers protects liberty as much as the explicit enumeration of rights. The Supreme Court has underscored this founding principle: "The ultimate purpose of this separation of powers is to protect the liberty and security of the governed." Metropolitan Wash. Airports Auth. v. Citizens for the Abatement of Aircraft Noise, Inc., 501 U.S. 252, 272 (1991). Thus, the textual allocation of responsibilities and the textual enumeration of rights are not dichotomous, because the textual separation of powers promotes a more profound understanding of our rights. For the judicial branch to trespass upon the exercise of the warmaking powers would be an infringement of the right to self-determination and self-governance at a time when the care of the common defense is most critical. This right of the people is no less a right because it is possessed collectively. . . .

B.

Despite the clear allocation of war powers to the political branches, judicial deference to executive decisions made in the name of war is not unlimited. . . .

. . . The Constitution is suffused with concern about how the state will wield its awesome power of forcible restraint. And this preoccupation was not accidental. Our forebears recognized that the power to detain could easily become destructive "if exerted without check or control" by an unrestrained executive free to "imprison, dispatch, or exile any man that was obnoxious to the government, by an instant declaration that such is their will and pleasure." 4 W. Blackstone, *Commentaries on the Laws of*

Chapter 13. Consequence Management: When the Worst Happens

England 349-50 (Cooley ed. 1899) (quoted in Duncan v. Louisiana, 391 U.S. 145, 151 (1968))).

The duty of the judicial branch to protect our individual freedoms does not simply cease whenever our military forces are committed by the political branches to armed conflict. The Founders "foresaw that troublous times would arise, when rulers and people would . . . seek by sharp and decisive measures to accomplish ends deemed just and proper; and that the principles of constitutional liberty would be in peril, unless established by irrepealable law." Ex Parte Milligan, 71 U.S. (4 Wall.) 2, 120 (1866). While that recognition does not dispose of this case, it does indicate one thing: The detention of United States citizens must be subject to judicial review. *See Hamdi II,* 296 F.3d at 283.

It is significant, moreover, that the form of relief sought by Hamdi is a writ of habeas corpus. In war as in peace, habeas corpus provides one of the firmest bulwarks against unconstitutional detentions. . . . While the scope of habeas review has expanded and contracted over the succeeding centuries, its essential function of assuring that restraint accords with the rule of law, not the whim of authority, remains unchanged. Hamdi's petition falls squarely within the Great Writ's purview, since he is an American citizen challenging his summary detention for reasons of state necessity.

C.

As the foregoing discussion reveals, the tensions within this case are significant. Such circumstances should counsel caution on the part of any court. Given the concerns discussed in the preceding sections, any broad or categorical holdings on enemy combatant designations would be especially inappropriate. We have no occasion, for example, to address the designation as an enemy combatant of an American citizen captured on American soil or the role that counsel might play in such a proceeding. *See, e.g.,* Padilla v. Bush, [233 F. Supp. 2d 564 (S.D.N.Y. 2002) (Supplement p. 69 *infra*)]. . . .

The safeguards that all Americans have come to expect in criminal prosecutions do not translate neatly to the arena of armed conflict. . . . For there is a "well-established power of the military to exercise jurisdiction over members of the armed forces, those directly connected with such forces, [and] enemy belligerents, prisoners of war, [and] others charged with violating the laws of war." Duncan v. Kahanamoku, 327 U.S. 304, 313-14 (1946) (footnotes omitted). As we emphasized in our prior decision, any judicial inquiry into Hamdi's status as an alleged enemy combatant in Afghanistan must reflect this deference as well as "a recognition that government has no more profound responsibility" than the protection of American citizens from further terrorist attacks. *Hamdi II,* 296 F.3d at 283.

In this regard, it is relevant that the detention of enemy combatants serves at least two vital purposes. First, detention prevents enemy combatants from rejoining the enemy and continuing to fight against America and its allies. "The object of capture is to prevent the captured individual from serving the enemy. He is disarmed and from then on he must be removed as completely as practicable from the front . . . ." In re Territo, 156 F.2d 142, 145 (9th Cir. 1946). In this respect, "captivity is neither a punishment nor an act of vengeance," but rather "a simple war measure." W. Winthrop, *Military Law and Precedents* 788 (2d ed. 1920). And the precautionary measure of disarming hostile forces for the duration of a conflict is routinely accomplished through detention rather than the initiation of criminal charges. To require otherwise would impose a singular burden upon our nation's conduct of war.

Second, detention in lieu of prosecution may relieve the burden on military commanders of litigating the circumstances of a capture halfway around the globe. This burden would not be inconsiderable and would run the risk of "saddling military decision-making with the panoply of encumbrances associated with civil litigation" during a period of armed conflict. *Hamdi II,* 296 F.3d at 283-84. As the Supreme Court has recognized, "[i]t would be difficult to devise more effective fettering of a field commander than to allow the very enemies he is ordered to reduce to submission to call him to account in his own civil courts and divert his efforts and attention from the military offensive abroad to the legal defensive at home." Johnson v. Eisentrager, 339 U.S. 763, 779 (1950).[4]

The judiciary is not at liberty to eviscerate detention interests directly derived from the war powers of Articles I and II. . . .

---

4. The government has contended that appointment of counsel for enemy combatants in the absence of charges would interfere with a third detention interest, that of gathering intelligence, by establishing an adversary relationship with the captor from the outset. *See Hamdi II,* 296 F.3d at 282 (expressing concern that the June 11 order of the district court "does not consider what effect petitioner's unmonitored access to counsel might have upon the government's ongoing gathering of intelligence"). That issue, however, is not presented in this appeal.

Chapter 13. Consequence Management: When the Worst Happens

III. . . .

. . . Hamdi and amici have . . . pressed two purely legal grounds for relief: 18 U.S.C. §4001(a) and Article 5 of the Geneva Convention. We now address them both.[5]

A.

18 U.S.C. §4001 regulates the detentions of United States citizens. It states . . . :

> (a) No citizen shall be imprisoned or otherwise detained by the United States except pursuant to an Act of Congress. . . .

Hamdi argues that there is no congressional sanction for his incarceration and that §4001(a) therefore prohibits his continued detention. We find this contention unpersuasive.

Even if Hamdi were right that §4001(a) requires Congressional authorization of his detention, Congress has, in the wake of the September 11 terrorist attacks, authorized the President to "use *all necessary and appropriate force* against those nations, organizations, or persons he determines planned, authorized, committed, or aided the terrorist attacks" or "harbored such organizations or persons." Authorization for Use of Military Force, Pub. L. No. 107-40, 115 Stat. 224 (Sept. 18, 2001) (emphasis added) [casebook p. 262]. As noted above, capturing and detaining enemy combatants is an inherent part of warfare; the "necessary and appropriate force" referenced in the congressional resolution necessarily includes the capture and detention of any and all hostile forces arrayed against our troops. Furthermore, Congress has specifically authorized the expenditure of funds for "the maintenance, pay, and allowances of prisoners of war [and] other persons in the custody of the [military] whose status is determined . . . to be similar to prisoners of war." 10 U.S.C. §956(5) (2002). It is difficult if not impossible to understand how Congress could make appropriations for the detention of persons "similar to prisoners of war" without also authorizing their detention in the first instance.

---

5. We reject at the outset one other claim that Hamdi has advanced in abbreviated form. He asserts that our approval of his continued detention means that the writ of habeas corpus has been unconstitutionally suspended. *See* U.S. Const. art. I, § 9. We find this unconvincing; the fact that we have not ordered the relief Hamdi requests is hardly equivalent to a suspension of the writ.

... Moreover, it has been clear since at least 1942 that "[c]itizenship in the United States of an enemy belligerent does not relieve him from the consequences of [his] belligerency." *Quirin,* 317 U.S. at 37. If Congress had intended to override this well-established precedent and provide American belligerents some immunity from capture and detention, it surely would have made its intentions explicit.

It is likewise significant that §4001(a) functioned principally to repeal the Emergency Detention Act. That statute had provided for the preventive "apprehension and detention" of individuals inside the United States "deemed likely to engage in espionage or sabotage" during "internal security emergencies." H.R. Rep. 92-116, at 2 (Apr. 6, 1971). Proponents of the repeal were concerned that the Emergency Detention Act might, inter alia, "permit[ ] a recurrence of the round ups which resulted in the detention of Americans of Japanese ancestry in 1941 and subsequently during World War II." *Id.* There is no indication that §4001(a) was intended to overrule the longstanding rule that an armed and hostile American citizen captured on the battlefield during wartime may be treated like the enemy combatant that he is. We therefore reject Hamdi's contention that §4001(a) bars his detention.

B.

Hamdi and amici also contend that Article 5 of the Geneva Convention applies to Hamdi's case and requires an initial formal determination of his status as an enemy belligerent "by a competent tribunal." Geneva Convention Relative to the Treatment of Prisoners of War, Aug. 12, 1949, art. 5, 6 U.S.T. 3316, 75 U.N.T.S. 135.

This argument falters also because the Geneva Convention is not self-executing. "Courts will only find a treaty to be self-executing if the document, as a whole, evidences an intent to provide a private right of action." Goldstar (Panama) v. United States, 967 F.2d 965, 968 (4th Cir. 1992). The Geneva Convention evinces no such intent. Certainly there is no explicit provision for enforcement by any form of private petition. And what discussion there is of enforcement focuses entirely on the vindication by diplomatic means of treaty rights inhering in sovereign nations. . . .

. . . Hamdi and the amici make much of the distinction between lawful and unlawful combatants, noting correctly that lawful combatants are not subject to punishment for their participation in a conflict. But for the purposes of this case, it is a distinction without a difference, since the option to detain until the cessation of hostilities belongs to the executive in either case. It is true that unlawful combatants are entitled to a proceeding before a military tribunal before they may be punished for the acts which render

Chapter 13. Consequence Management: When the Worst Happens 65

their belligerency unlawful. *Quirin,* 317 U.S. at 31. But they are also subject to mere detention in precisely the same way that lawful prisoners of war are. *Id.* The fact that Hamdi might be an unlawful combatant in no way means that the executive is required to inflict every consequence of that status on him. The Geneva Convention certainly does not require such treatment. . . .

IV.

. . . [W]e conclude that Hamdi's petition fails as a matter of law. It follows that the government should not be compelled to produce the materials described in the district court's August 16 order.

We also note that the order, if enforced, would present formidable practical difficulties. The district court indicated that its production request might well be only an initial step in testing the factual basis of Hamdi's enemy combatant status. The court plainly did not preclude making further production demands upon the government, even suggesting that it might "bring Hamdi before [the court] to inquire about [his] statements." . . .

A review of the court's August 16 order reveals the risk of "stand[ing] the warmaking powers of Articles I and II on their heads," *Hamdi II,* 296 F.3d at 284. The district court, for example, ordered the government to produce all Hamdi's statements and notes from interviews. Yet it is precisely such statements, relating to a detainee's activities in Afghanistan, that may contain the most sensitive and the most valuable information for our forces in the field. The risk created by this order is that judicial involvement would proceed, increment by increment, into an area where the political branches have been assigned by law a preeminent role.

The district court further ordered the government to produce a list of all interrogators who have questioned Hamdi, including their names and addresses and the dates of the interviews, copies of any statements by members of the Northern Alliance regarding Hamdi's surrender, and a list that includes the date of Hamdi's capture and all the dates and locations of his subsequent detention. Once again, however, litigation cannot be the driving force in effectuating and recording wartime detentions. The military has been charged by Congress and the executive with winning a war, not prevailing in a possible court case. Complicating the matter even further is the fact that Hamdi was originally captured by Northern Alliance forces, with whom American forces were generally allied. The district court's insistence that statements by Northern Alliance members be produced cannot help but place a strain on multilateral efforts during wartime. . . .

Viewed in their totality, the implications of the district court's August 16 production order could not be more serious. The factual inquiry upon which Hamdi would lead us, if it did not entail disclosure of sensitive intelligence, might require an excavation of facts buried under the rubble of war. The cost of such an inquiry in terms of the efficiency and morale of American forces cannot be disregarded. Some of those with knowledge of Hamdi's detention may have been slain or injured in battle. Others might have to be diverted from active and ongoing military duties of their own. The logistical effort to acquire evidence from far away battle zones might be substantial. And these efforts would profoundly unsettle the constitutional balance.

For the foregoing reasons, the court's August 16 production request cannot stand.

V. . . .

[Having concluded that there were no purely legal impediments to military detention and that the district court's production order could not stand, the panel then considered whether a remand was necessary for a factual inquiry to decide whether Hamdi was a combatant subject to military detention.]

Generally speaking, in order to fulfill our responsibilities under Article III to review a petitioner's allegation that he is being detained by American authorities in violation of the rights afforded him under the United States Constitution, we must first determine the source of the authority for the executive to detain the individual. Once the source of the authority is identified, we then look at the justification given to determine whether it constitutes a legitimate exercise of that authority.

A.

Here the government has identified the source of the authority to detain Hamdi as originating in Article II, Section 2 of the Constitution, wherein the President is given the war power. We have already emphasized that the standard of review of enemy combatant detentions must be a deferential one when the detainee was captured abroad in a zone of combat operations. The President "is best prepared to exercise the military judgment attending the capture of alleged combatants." *Hamdi II*, 296 F.3d at 283. Thus, in *Quirin*, the Supreme Court stated in no uncertain terms that detentions "ordered by the President in the declared exercise of his powers as Commander in Chief of the Army in time of war and of grave public danger" should not "be set aside by the courts without the clear conviction that they are in conflict with the Constitution or laws of Congress constitutionally enacted." *Quirin,* 317 U.S. at 25.

This deferential posture, however, only comes into play after we ascertain that the challenged decision is one legitimately made pursuant to the war powers. . . . [I]n this case, the government has voluntarily submitted – and urged us to review – an affidavit from Michael Mobbs, Special Advisor to the Under Secretary of Defense for Policy, describing what the government contends were the circumstances leading to Hamdi's designation as an enemy combatant under Article II's war power.

The Mobbs affidavit consists of two pages and nine paragraphs in which Mobbs states that he was "substantially involved with matters related to the detention of enemy combatants in the current war against the al Qaeda terrorists and those who support and harbor them." . . .

To be sure, a capable attorney could challenge the hearsay nature of the Mobbs declaration and probe each and every paragraph for incompleteness or inconsistency, as the district court attempted to do. The court's approach, however, had a signal flaw. We are not here dealing with a defendant who has been indicted on criminal charges in the exercise of the executive's law enforcement powers. We are dealing with the executive's assertion of its power to detain under the war powers of Article II. *See Eisentrager,* 339 U.S. at 793 (Black, J., dissenting) ("[I]t is no 'crime' to be a soldier."). To transfer the instinctive skepticism, so laudable in the defense of criminal charges, to the review of executive branch decisions premised on military determinations made in the field carries the inordinate risk of a constitutionally problematic intrusion into the most basic responsibilities of a coordinate branch. . . .

. . . Asking the executive to provide more detailed factual assertions would be to wade further into the conduct of war than we consider appropriate and is unnecessary to a meaningful judicial review of this question.

B.

. . . We hold that no evidentiary hearing or factual inquiry on our part is necessary or proper, because it is undisputed that Hamdi was captured in a zone of active combat operations in a foreign country and because any inquiry must be circumscribed to avoid encroachment into the military affairs entrusted to the executive branch. . . .

1. . . . We cannot stress too often the constitutional implications presented on the face of Hamdi's petition. The constitutional allocation of war powers affords the President extraordinarily broad authority as

Commander in Chief and compels courts to assume a deferential posture in reviewing exercises of this authority. And, while the Constitution assigns courts the duty generally to review executive detentions that are alleged to be illegal, the Constitution does not specifically contemplate any role for courts in the conduct of war, or in foreign policy generally. Indeed, Article III courts are ill-positioned to police the military's distinction between those in the arena of combat who should be detained and those who should not. . . .

. . . Any effort to ascertain the facts concerning the petitioner's conduct while amongst the nation's enemies would entail an unacceptable risk of obstructing war efforts authorized by Congress and undertaken by the executive branch.

2. Hamdi contends that, although international law and the laws of this country might generally allow for the detention of an individual captured on the battlefield, these laws must vary in his case because he is an American citizen now detained on American soil. As an American citizen, Hamdi would be entitled to the due process protections normally found in the criminal justice system, including the right to meet with counsel, if he had been charged with a crime. But as we have previously pointed out, Hamdi has not been charged with any crime. He is being held as an enemy combatant pursuant to the well-established laws and customs of war. . . .

. . . At least where it is undisputed that he was present in a zone of active combat operations, we are satisfied that the Constitution does not entitle him to a searching review of the factual determinations underlying his seizure there. . . .

C.

Finally, we address Hamdi's contention that even if his detention was at one time lawful, it is no longer so because the relevant hostilities have reached an end. In his brief, Hamdi alleges that the government "confuses the international armed conflict that allegedly authorized Hamdi's detention in the first place with an on-going fight against individuals whom Respondents refuse to recognize as 'belligerents' under international law." *Id*. at 53-54. Whether the timing of a cessation of hostilities is justiciable is far from clear. The executive branch is also in the best position to appraise the status of a conflict, and the cessation of hostilities would seem no less a matter of political competence than the initiation of them. *See* United States v. The Three Friends, 166 U.S. 1, 63 (1897). In any case, we need not reach this issue here. The government notes that American troops are still on the ground in Afghanistan, dismantling the terrorist infrastructure in the very country where Hamdi was captured and engaging in reconstruction efforts which may prove dangerous in their own right. Because under the most circumscribed definition of conflict hostilities have not yet reached their end, this argument is without merit.

VI. . . .

The events of September 11 have left their indelible mark. It is not wrong even in the dry annals of judicial opinion to mourn those who lost their lives that terrible day. Yet we speak in the end not from sorrow or anger, but from the conviction that separation of powers takes on special significance when the nation itself comes under attack. Hamdi's status as a citizen, as important as that is, cannot displace our constitutional order or the place of the courts within the Framer's scheme. Judicial review does not disappear during wartime, but the review of battlefield captures in overseas conflicts is a highly deferential one. That is why, for reasons stated, the judgment must be reversed and the petition dismissed. It is so ordered.

Padilla v. Bush
United States District Court, Southern District of New York, 2002
233 F. Supp. 2d 564

MUKASEY, District Judge. Petitioner in this case, Jose Padilla, was arrested on May 8, 2002, in Chicago, on a material witness warrant issued by this court pursuant to 18 U.S.C. §3144 to enforce a subpoena to secure Padilla's testimony before a grand jury in this District. His arrest and initial detention were carried out by the U.S. Department of Justice. As the result of events described below – including the President's designation of Padilla as an enemy combatant associated with a terrorist network called al Qaeda – Padilla is now detained, without formal charges against him or the prospect of release after the giving of testimony before a grand jury, in the custody of the U.S. Department of Defense at the Consolidated Naval Brig in Charleston, South Carolina.

Through his attorney, Donna R. Newman, acting as next friend, Padilla has petitioned pursuant to 28 U.S.C. §2241, seeking relief in the nature of habeas corpus, challenging the lawfulness of his detention, and seeking an order directing that he be permitted to consult with counsel. . . . [The court found that Newman had standing, as Padilla's next friend, to file the petition, and that it had personal jurisdiction over the Secretary of Defense.]

For the reasons set forth below, the parties' applications and motions are resolved as follows: . . . (iii) the President is authorized under the Constitution and by law to direct the military to detain enemy combatants in the circumstances present here, such that Padilla's detention is not *per se* unlawful; (iv) Padilla may consult with counsel in aid of pursuing this petition, under conditions that will minimize the likelihood that he can use his lawyers as unwilling intermediaries for the transmission of information to others and may, if he chooses, submit facts and argument to the court in aid of his petition; (v) to resolve the issue of whether Padilla was lawfully detained on the facts present here, the court will examine only whether the President had some evidence to support his finding that Padilla was an enemy combatant, and whether that evidence has been mooted by events subsequent to his detention; the court will not at this time use the document submitted *in camera* to determine whether the government has met that standard.

I. FACTUAL BACKGROUND

The immediate and legal predicate for this case lies in the September 11, 2001 attacks on this country, and the government's response. . . .

On September 14, 2001, by reason of these attacks, the President declared a state of national emergency. On September 18, 2001, Congress passed Public Law No. 107-40 . . . entitled . . . Authorization for Use of Military Force, Pub. Law No. 107-40, 115 Stat. 224 (2001) [casebook p. 262, Note 7]. . . .

As previously noted, on May 8, 2002, this court, acting on an application by the Justice Department pursuant to 18 U.S.C. §3144, . . . found that Padilla appeared to have knowledge of facts relevant to a grand jury investigation into the September 11 attacks. That investigation included an ongoing inquiry into the activities of al Qaeda, an organization believed to be responsible for the September 11 attacks, among others, and to be committed to and involved in planning further attacks. On May 15, 2002, following Padilla's removal from Chicago to New York, where he was detained in the custody of the Justice Department . . . he appeared before this court, and Donna R. Newman, Esq. was appointed to represent him. After Newman had conferred with Padilla . . . Padilla, represented by Newman, moved to vacate the warrant. . . .

. . . [O]n June 9, 2002, the government notified the court *ex parte* that it was withdrawing the subpoena. Pursuant to the government's request, the court signed an order vacating the warrant. At that time, the government disclosed that the President had designated Padilla an enemy combatant, on grounds discussed more fully below, and directed the Secretary of Defense,

Chapter 13. Consequence Management: When the Worst Happens

respondent Donald Rumsfeld, to detain Padilla. The government disclosed to the court as well that the Department of Defense would take custody of Padilla forthwith, and transfer him to South Carolina, as in fact happened.

. . . Newman filed a habeas corpus petition pursuant to 28 U.S.C. §2241. . . . Newman has averred that she was told she would not be permitted to visit Padilla at the South Carolina facility, or to speak with him; she was told she could write to Padilla, but that he might not receive the correspondence.

. . . No criminal charges have been filed against Padilla.

The President's order, dated June 9, 2002 (the "June 9 Order"), is attached, in redacted form, to the government's dismissal motion, and sets forth in summary fashion the President's findings with respect to Padilla. Attached as well is a declaration of Michael H. Mobbs ("Mobbs Declaration"), who is employed by the Department of Defense. The Mobbs Declaration sets forth a redacted version of facts provided to the President as the basis for the conclusions set forth in the June 9 Order. In addition to the redacted summary contained in the Mobbs Declaration, the government has submitted, under seal, an unredacted version of information provided to the President ("Sealed Mobbs Declaration"). As set forth more fully below, the government has argued that the Mobbs Declaration is sufficient to establish the correctness of the President's findings contained in the June 9 Order, although it has made the Sealed Mobbs Declaration available to the court to remedy any perceived insufficiency in the Mobbs Declaration. However, the government has maintained that the Sealed Mobbs Declaration must remain confidential. The government has taken the position that it would withdraw the Sealed Mobbs Declaration sooner than disclose its contents to defense counsel.

The June 9 Order is addressed to the Secretary of Defense, and includes seven numbered paragraphs setting forth the President's conclusion that Padilla is an enemy combatant, and, in summary form, the basis for that conclusion, including that Padilla: is "closely associated with al Qaeda," engaged in "hostile and war-like acts" including "preparation for acts of international terrorism" directed at this country, possesses information that would be helpful in preventing al Qaeda attacks, and represents "a continuing, present and grave danger to the national security of the United States." In addition, the June 9 Order directs Secretary Rumsfeld to detain Padilla.

The Mobbs Declaration states that Padilla was born in New York and convicted in Chicago, before he turned 18, of murder. Released from prison after he turned 18, Padilla was convicted in Florida in 1991 of a weapons charge. After his release from prison on that charge, Padilla moved to Egypt, took the name Abdullah al Muhajir, and is alleged to have traveled also to Saudi Arabia and Afghanistan. In 2001, while in Afghanistan, Padilla is alleged to have approached "senior Usama Bin Laden lieutenant Abu Zubaydeh" and proposed, among other things, stealing radioactive material within the United States so as to build, and detonate a "'radiological dispersal device' (also known as a 'dirty bomb') within the United States." Padilla is alleged to have done research on such a project at an al Qaeda safehouse in Lahore, Pakistan, and to have discussed that and other proposals for terrorist acts within the United States with al Qaeda officials he met in Karachi, Pakistan, on a trip he made at the behest of Abu Zubaydah. One of the unnamed confidential sources referred to in the Mobbs Declaration said he did not believe Padilla was actually a member of al Qaeda, but Mobbs emphasizes that Padilla had "extended contacts with senior Al Qaeda members and operatives" and that he "acted under the direction of [Abu] Zubaydah and other senior Al Qaeda operatives, received training from Al Qaeda operatives in furtherance of terrorist activities, and was sent to the United States to conduct reconnaissance and/or conduct other attacks on their behalf." . . .

Dealing with the contents of the Sealed Mobbs Declaration is problematic. Padilla argues that I should not consider it at all, at least unless his lawyers have access to it and, he argues, he has an opportunity to respond to its contents. The government argues that I must not disclose it, but that I need not consider it because the redacted version of what the President was told, as set forth in the Mobbs Declaration, is enough to justify the June 9 Order, unless for some reason I think otherwise, in which case I am invited to examine it *in camera*. . . .

Secretary Rumsfeld distinguished as follows the government's handling of Padilla from its handling of the usual case of one charged with breaking the law:

> It seems to me that the problem in the United States is that we have – we are in a certain mode. Our normal procedure is that if somebody does something unlawful, illegal against our system of government, that the first thing we want to do is apprehend them, then try them in a court and then punish them. In this case that is not our first interest.
>
> Our interest is to – we are not interested in trying him at the moment; we are not interested in punishing him at the moment. We are interested in finding out what he knows. Here is a person who unambiguously was interested in radiation weapons and terrorist activity, and was in league with al Qaeda. Now our job, as responsible government officials, is to do everything possible to find out what that person knows, and see if we can't help our country or other countries.

[News Briefing, Department of Defense (June 12, 2002), 2002 WL 22026773.] . . .

It is not disputed that Padilla is held incommunicado, and specifically that he has not been permitted to consult with Newman or any other counsel. . . .

IV. THE LAWFULNESS OF PADILLA'S DETENTION

The basic question dividing the parties is whether Padilla is lawfully detained. Like the question of whether this court has jurisdiction, that basic question unfolds into subsidiary questions: Does the President have the authority to designate as an enemy combatant an American citizen captured on American soil, and, through the Secretary of Defense, to detain him for the duration of armed conflict with al Qaeda? If so, can the President exercise that authority without violating 18 U.S.C. §4001(a), which bars the detention of American citizens "except pursuant to an Act of Congress"? If so, by whatever standard this court must apply – itself a separate issue – is the evidence adduced by the government sufficient to justify the detention of Padilla? . . .

For the reasons set forth below, the answer to the first two of those questions is yes; a definitive answer to the third of those questions must await a further submission from Padilla, should he choose to make one, although the court will examine only whether there was some evidence to support the President's finding, and whether that evidence has been mooted by events subsequent to Padilla's detention.

A. *The President's Authority To Order That Padilla Be Detained As An Enemy Combatant*

Neither Padilla nor any of the amici denies directly the authority of the President to order the seizure and detention of enemy combatants in a time of war. Rather, they seek to distinguish this case from cases in which the President may make such an order on the grounds that this is not a time of war, and therefore the President may not use his powers as Commander in Chief or apply the laws of war to Padilla, and that Padilla in any event must be treated differently because he is an American citizen captured on American soil where the courts are functioning.

The claim by petitioner and the amici that this is not a time of war has two prongs: First, because Congress did not declare war on Afghanistan, the only nation state against which United States forces have taken direct action, the measures sanctioned during declared wars, principally in Ex Parte Quirin, 317 U.S. 1, discussed below, are not available here. Second, because the current conflict is with al Qaeda, which is essentially an international criminal organization that lacks clear corporeal definition, the conflict can have no clear end, and thus the detention of enemy combatants is potentially indefinite and therefore unconstitutional. For the reasons discussed below, neither prong of the argument withstands scrutiny.

The first prong of the argument – that we are not in a war and that only Congress can declare war – does not engage the real issue in this case, which concerns what powers the President may exercise in the present circumstances. Even assuming that a court can pronounce when a "war" exists, in the sense in which that word is used in the Constitution, *cf.* Bas v. Tingy, 4 U.S. (4 Dall.) 37, 42 (1800) (determining whether France, with which the United States had engaged in an undeclared naval war, was an "enemy" within the meaning of a prize statute, but noting that whether there was a war in a constitutional sense was irrelevant: "Besides, it may be asked, why should the rate of salvage be different in such a war as the present, from the salvage in a war more solemn [*i.e.,* declared] or general?"), a formal declaration of war is not necessary in order for the executive to exercise its constitutional authority to prosecute an armed conflict – particularly when, as on September 11, the United States is attacked. In The Prize Cases, 67 U.S. (2 Black) 635 (1862), the Supreme Court rejected a challenge to the President's authority to impose a blockade on the secessionist states – an act of war – when there had been no declaration of war. . . . Here, I agree completely with Judge Silberman who, after examining and quoting from *The Prize Cases,* wrote as follows:

> I read the *Prize Cases* to stand for the proposition that the President has independent authority to repel aggressive acts by third parties even without specific congressional authorization, and courts may not review the level of force selected.

Campbell v. Clinton, 203 F.3d 19, 27 (D.C. Cir. 2000) (Silberman, J., concurring) . . . .

The conclusion that the President may exercise his powers as Commander in Chief without a declaration of war is borne out not only by legal precedent, but also by even the briefest contemplation of our history. When one considers the sheer number of military campaigns undertaken during this country's history, declarations of war are the exception rather than the rule, beginning with the undeclared but Congressionally authorized naval war against France in the 1790's referred to in Bas v. Tingy, cited above. Taking into account only the modern era, the last declared war was World War II. Since then, this country has fought the Korean War, the Viet Nam War, the Persian Gulf War, and the Kosovo bombing campaign, as

Chapter 13. Consequence Management: When the Worst Happens 75

well as other military engagements in Lebanon, Haiti, Grenada and Somalia, to cite a random and by no means exhaustive list, with no appellate authority holding that a declaration of war was necessary. When confronted with challenges to the Viet Nam War, several appellate courts held specifically that no declaration of war was necessary.

Further, even if Congressional authorization were deemed necessary, the Joint Resolution, passed by both houses of Congress, authorizes the President to use necessary and appropriate force in order, among other things, "to prevent any future acts of international terrorism against the United States," and thereby engages the President's full powers as Commander in Chief. Authorization for Use of Military Force §2(a). . . .

The question of when the conflict with al Qaeda may end is one that need not be addressed. So long as American troops remain on the ground in Afghanistan and Pakistan in combat with and pursuit of al Qaeda fighters, there is no basis for contradicting the President's repeated assertions that the conflict has not ended. *See* Ludecke v. Watkins, 335 U.S. 160, 167-69 (1948) (deferring to the President's position that a state of war continued to exist despite Germany's surrender to the Allies). At some point in the future, when operations against al Qaeda fighters end, or the operational capacity of al Qaeda is effectively destroyed, there may be occasion to debate the legality of continuing to hold prisoners based on their connection to al Qaeda, assuming such prisoners continue to be held at that time.

. . . [I]nsofar as [Padilla's] argument assumes that indefinite confinement of one not convicted of a crime is *per se* unconstitutional, that assumption is simply wrong. In Kansas v. Hendricks, 521 U.S. 346 (1997), the Court upheld Kansas's Sexually Violent Predator Act, providing for civil commitment of those who, due to "mental abnormality" or "personality disorder" are likely to commit sexually predatory acts. Rejecting the argument that the statute imposed criminal sanctions in the guise of a civil remedy, the Court noted that "commitment under the Act does not implicate either of the two primary objectives of criminal punishment: retribution or deterrence." *Id.* at 361-62. . . . *See also* United States v. Salerno, 481 U.S. 739, 748 (1987) ("We have repeatedly held that the Government's regulatory interest in community safety can, in appropriate circumstances, outweigh an individual's liberty interest. For example, in times of war and insurrection, when society's interest is at its peak, the Government may detain individuals whom the Government believes to be dangerous."); Moyer v. Peabody, 212 U.S. 78, 84 (1909) (upholding the detention of a union president without charge during an insurrection, reasoning: "Such arrests are not necessarily for punishment but are by way of precaution, to prevent the exercise of hostile power"). To be sure, the standard of proof in some of those cases may well have been higher than the standard ultimately will be found to be in this case, but the point is that there is no *per se* ban. . . .

. . . Before examining directly the issue of the President's authority, it is necessary to examine what the designation "enemy combatant" means in this case. The laws of war draw a fundamental distinction between lawful and unlawful combatants. Lawful combatants may be held as prisoners of war, but are immune from criminal prosecution by their captors for belligerent acts that do not constitute war crimes. *See* United States v. Lindh, 212 F. Supp. 2d 541, 553 (E.D. Va. 2002) (citing numerous authorities).

Four criteria generally determine the conditions an armed force and its members must meet in order to be considered lawful combatants:

> (1) To be commanded by a person responsible for his subordinates; (2) To have a fixed distinctive emblem recognizable at a distance; (3) To carry arms openly; and (4) To conduct their operations in accordance with the laws and customs of War.

Convention Respecting the Laws and Customs of War on Land, with Annex of Regulations, Oct. 18, 1907, Annex art. 1, 36 Stat. 2277, T.S. No. 539 (Jan. 26, 1910) (the "Hague Convention" and the "Hague Regulations"). Those who do not meet those criteria, including saboteurs and guerrillas, may not claim prisoner of war status. *See Quirin,* 317 U.S. at 31 (citing authorities for the proposition that unlawful combatants are "offenders against the law of war" and may be tried by military tribunals). . . .

Although unlawful combatants, unlike prisoners of war, may be tried and punished by military tribunals, there is no basis to impose a requirement that they be punished. Rather, their detention for the duration of hostilities is supportable – again, logically and legally – on the same ground that the detention of prisoners of war is supportable: to prevent them from rejoining the enemy. . . .

As noted, in the June 9 Order, the President designated Padilla an "enemy combatant" based on his alleged association with al Qaeda and on an alleged plan undertaken as part of that association. The point of the protracted discussion immediately above is simply to support what should be an obvious conclusion: when the President designated Padilla an "enemy combatant," he necessarily meant that Padilla was an unlawful combatant, acting as an associate of a terrorist organization whose operations do not meet the four criteria necessary to confer lawful combatant status on its members and adherents. *See Quirin,* 317 U.S. at 31 (describing an unlawful

Chapter 13. Consequence Management: When the Worst Happens

combatant as, *inter alia,* one "who without uniform comes secretly through the lines for the purpose of waging war by destruction of life or property"). . . .

. . . Padilla and the amici argue that, regardless of what treatment is permitted under the Third Geneva Convention and otherwise for unlawful combatants, the Constitution forbids indefinite detention of a citizen captured on American soil so long as "the courts are open and their process unobstructed," Ex parte Milligan, 71 U.S. (4 Wall.) 2 (1866). . . .

Milligan, however, received a narrow reading in *Quirin,* a case on which the government, not surprisingly, places heavy reliance. . . . Because the *Quirin* Court found that the German saboteurs were not only attempting to harm the United States during an armed conflict but doing so as persons associated with an enemy's armed forces, the Court concluded that the saboteurs, unlike Milligan, could be treated as unlawful combatants. Padilla, like the saboteurs, is alleged to be in active association with an enemy with whom the United States is at war.

Although the particular issue before the Court in *Quirin* – whether those petitioners could be tried by a military tribunal – is not precisely the same as the one now before this court – whether Padilla may be held without trial, the logic of *Quirin* bears strongly on this case. First, *Quirin* recognized the distinction between lawful and unlawful combatants, and the different treatment to which each is potentially subject:

> By universal agreement and practice the law of war draws a distinction between . . . lawful and unlawful combatants. Lawful combatants are subject to capture and detention as prisoners of war by opposing military forces. Unlawful combatants are likewise subject to capture and detention, but in addition they are subject to trial and punishment by military tribunals for acts which render their belligerency unlawful.

Id. at 30-31. . . . Although the issue of detention alone was not before the Court in *Quirin,* I read the quoted sentence to mean that as between detention alone, and trial by a military tribunal with exposure to the penalty actually meted out to petitioners in *Quirin* – death – or, at the least, exposure to a sentence of imprisonment intended to punish and deter, the Court regarded detention alone, with the sole aim of preventing the detainee from rejoining hostile forces – a consequence visited upon captured lawful combatants – as certainly the lesser of the consequences an unlawful combatant could face. . . .

The *Quirin* Court found it "unnecessary for present purposes to determine to what extent the President as Commander in Chief has constitutional power to create military commissions without the support of

Congressional legislation. For here Congress has authorized trial of offenses against the law of war before such commissions." *Quirin,* 317 U.S. at 29. However, the Court did suggest that the President's decision to try the saboteurs before a military tribunal rested at least in part on an exercise of Presidential authority under Article II of the Constitution:

> By his order creating the present Commission [the President] has undertaken to exercise the authority conferred upon him by Congress, and also such authority as the Constitution itself gives the Commander in Chief, to direct the performance of those functions which may constitutionally be performed by the military arm of the nation in time of war.

Id. at 28.

Here, the basis for the President's authority to order the detention of an unlawful combatant arises both from the terms of the Joint Resolution, and from his constitutional authority as Commander in Chief as set forth in *The Prize Cases* and other authority discussed above. . . .

B. *Is Padilla's Detention Barred by Statute?*

Whatever may be the President's authority to act in the absence of a specific limiting legislative enactment, Padilla and the amici argue that 18 U.S.C. §4001(a) bars his confinement in the circumstances present here . . . . However, as set forth below, §4001(a), which by its terms applies to Padilla, bars confinement only in the absence of congressional authorization, and there has been congressional authorization here . . . .

Padilla's principal statutory argument is based on 18 U.S.C. §4001(a), which is broad and categorical:

> No citizen shall be imprisoned or otherwise detained by the United States except pursuant to an Act of Congress.

18 U.S.C. §4001(a) (2000); *see* Howe v. Smith, 452 U.S. 473, 480 n. 3 (1981) ("[T]he plain language of §4001(a) proscrib[es] detention *of any kind* by the United States, absent a congressional grant of authority to detain.") (emphasis in original).

To avoid the reach of that statute, the government appears to lean heavily on statutory construction arguments that fail to confront the plain language of the statute, and to rest rather lightly on what seems to me the more persuasive position: that Padilla in fact is detained "pursuant to an Act of Congress." Thus, the government argues that reading §4001(a) to cover Padilla's detention would bring that section in conflict with Article II,

Chapter 13. Consequence Management: When the Worst Happens 79

section 2, clause 1 of the Constitution, which makes the President "Commander in Chief of the Army and Navy of the United States," U.S. Const., art. 2, §2, cl. 1, and has been interpreted to grant the President independent authority to respond to an armed attack against the United States. *See* The Prize Cases, 67 U.S. at 668, 2 Black 635 ("If a war be made by invasion of a foreign nation, the President is not only authorized but bound to resist force by force . . . without waiting for any special legislative authority.").

The government suggests that because reading the statute to impinge on the President's Article II powers, including detention of enemy combatants, creates a danger that the statute might be found unconstitutional as applied to the present case, a court should read the statute so as not to cover detention of enemy combatants, applying the canon that a statute should be read so as to avoid constitutional difficulty.

However, this doctrine of constitutional avoidance "'has no application in the absence of statutory ambiguity.'" HUD v. Rucker, 535 U.S. 125 (2002) (quoting United States v. Oakland Cannabis Buyers' Cooperative, 532 U.S. 483, 494 (2001)). . . . There is no ambiguity here. The plain language of the statute encompasses all detentions of United States citizens. Therefore, the constitutional avoidance canon cannot affect how the statute is read. . . .

. . . The statute permits detention of an American citizen "pursuant to an Act of Congress." 18 U.S.C. §4001(a) (2000). If the Military Force Authorization passed and signed on September 18, 2001, is an "Act of Congress," and if it authorizes Padilla's detention, then perforce the statute has not been violated here. . . .

Principally because the Joint Resolution complies with all constitutional requirements for an Act of Congress, it should be regarded for purposes of §4001(a) as an "Act of Congress."

The authority conferred by the Joint Resolution itself is broad. It authorizes the President to "use all necessary and appropriate force against those . . . organizations, or persons he determines planned, authorized, committed or aided the terrorist attacks that occurred on September 11, 2001 . . . in order to prevent any future acts of international terrorism against the United States by such . . . organizations or persons." Authorization for Use of Military Force, Pub. Law No. 107-40, §2(a), 115 Stat. 224, 224 (2001). This language authorizes action against not only those connected to the subject organizations who are directly responsible for the September 11 attacks, but also against those who would engage in "future acts of international terrorism" as part of "such . . . organizations." *Id.* . . . Accordingly, the detention of Padilla is not barred by 18 U.S.C. §4001(a); nor, as discussed above, is it otherwise barred as a matter of law.

V. CONSULTATION WITH COUNSEL

The government has not disputed Padilla's right to challenge his detention by means of a habeas corpus petition. Although Padilla has the ability, through his lawyer, to challenge the government's naked legal right to hold him as an unlawful combatant on any set of facts whatsoever, he has no ability to make fact-based arguments because, as is not disputed, he has been held incommunicado during his confinement at the Consolidated Naval Brig in Charleston, and has not been permitted to consult with counsel. . . .

The habeas corpus statutes do not explicitly provide a right to counsel for a petitioner in Padilla's circumstances, but 18 U.S.C. §3006A(2)(B) permits a court to which a §2241 petition is addressed to appoint counsel for the petitioner if the court determines that "the interests of justice so require." 18 U.S.C. §3006A(2)(B) (2000). I have already so determined, and have continued the appointment of Newman and appointed also Andrew Patel, Esq., as co-counsel.

Of course, Padilla has no Sixth Amendment right to counsel in this proceeding. The Sixth Amendment grants that right to the "accused" in a "criminal proceeding"; Padilla is in the custody of the Department of Defense; there is no "criminal proceeding" in which Padilla is detained; therefore, the Sixth Amendment does not speak to Padilla's situation. . . .

The Due Process Clause of the Fifth Amendment states that "[n]o person . . . shall be deprived of life, liberty, or property, without due process of law." U.S. Const., amend. V. . . . Finding guidance in the due process clause would require, at a minimum, locating the delicate balance between private and public interests that is the test for finding a due process right, as set forth in Mathews v. Eldridge, 424 U.S. 319 (1976) . . . . However, as explained below, the provisions and characteristics of the habeas corpus statute and remedy discussed above, and the court's power under the All Writs Act, 28 U.S.C. §1651(a) (2000), to issue writs in aid of its jurisdiction, provide a statutory basis for decision. Considerations of prudence require that a court avoid a constitutional basis for decision when there exists a non-constitutional alternative.

Part of that non-constitutional alternative lies in the provisions of the habeas corpus statute, and the characteristics of the remedy, discussed above, which make it clear that Congress intended habeas corpus petitioners to have an opportunity to present and contest facts, and courts to have the flexibility to permit them to do so under proper safeguards. Padilla's need to consult with a lawyer to help him do what the statute permits him to do is obvious. He is held incommunicado at a military facility. His lawyer has been told that there is no guarantee even that her correspondence to him

Chapter 13. Consequence Management: When the Worst Happens   81

would get through. . . . It would frustrate the purpose of the procedure Congress established in habeas corpus cases, and of the remedy itself, to leave Padilla with no practical means whatever for following that procedure. . . .

The government has argued that affording access to counsel would "jeopardize the two core purposes of detaining enemy combatants – gathering intelligence about the enemy, and preventing the detainee from aiding in any further attacks against America." This would happen, the government argues, because access to counsel would interfere with questioning, and because al Qaeda operatives are trained to use third parties as intermediaries to pass messages to fellow terrorists, even if "[t]he intermediaries may be unaware that they are being so used."

However, access to counsel need be granted only for purposes of presenting facts to the court in connection with this petition if Padilla wishes to do so; no general right to counsel in connection with questioning has been hypothesized here, and thus the interference with interrogation would be minimal or nonexistent. . . . Although the government presents facts showing that Padilla had contact with and was acting on behalf of al Qaeda, there is nothing to indicate that Padilla in particular was trained to transmit information in the way the government suggests, or that he had information to transmit. . . . Fourth, there is no reason that military personnel cannot monitor Padilla's contacts with counsel, so long as those who participate in the monitoring are insulated from any activity in connection with this petition, or in connection with a future criminal prosecution of Padilla, if there should ever be one. . . .

. . . [R]espondent Secretary Rumsfeld will be directed to permit Padilla to consult with counsel solely for the purpose of submitting to the court facts bearing upon his petition, under such conditions as the parties may agree to, or, absent agreement, such conditions as the court may direct so as to foreclose, so far as possible, the danger that Padilla will use his attorneys for the purpose of conveying information to others.

VI. THE STANDARD APPLICABLE TO THIS COURT'S REVIEW AND THE FACTS THE COURT MAY CONSIDER

Before Padilla consults with counsel for the purpose of submitting facts to the court in aid of his petition, it would seem essential for him to know what standard the court will apply in determining whether whatever facts the government has presented are sufficient to warrant the finding in the President's June 9 Order that Padilla is an unlawful combatant. In addition, it would be helpful for Padilla to know, at least in a general sense, what the court will consider in that calculus other than what appears in the Mobbs

Declaration – in particular, whether the court will consider the Sealed Mobbs Declaration. Unless he has some idea as to both of these subjects, he cannot decide what sort of factual presentation he must make, or indeed whether he wishes to stand mute rather than try to present any facts at all. . . .

A. *Deference Due the President's Determination*

Padilla does not seem to dispute that courts owe considerable deference, as a general matter, to the acts and orders of the political branches – the President and Congress – in matters relating to foreign policy, national security, or military affairs. Nor could he. . . .

Padilla insists that this court conduct a "searching inquiry" into the factual basis for the President's determination that Padilla is an enemy combatant, lest the court "rubber stamp" the June 9 Order and thereby enforce a "Presidential whim." In essence, Padilla argues that he is entitled to a trial on the issue of whether he is an unlawful combatant or not.

However, as set forth above, Padilla has lost the legal arguments he relies on to remove this case from the reach of the principles described by the Fourth Circuit in *Hamdi,* cited above. The President, for the reasons set forth above, has both constitutional and statutory authority to exercise the powers of Commander in Chief, including the power to detain unlawful combatants, and it matters not that Padilla is a United States citizen captured on United States soil. . . . In the decision to detain Padilla as an unlawful combatant, for the reasons set forth [in Justice Jackson's concurring opinion in the *Steel Seizure Case*], the President is operating at maximum authority, under both the Constitution and the Joint Resolution.

. . . [I]t would be a mistake to create the impression that there is a lush and vibrant jurisprudence governing these matters. There isn't. *Quirin* offers no guidance regarding the standard to be applied in making the threshold determination that a habeas corpus petitioner is an unlawful combatant. Because the facts in *Quirin* were stipulated, *see Quirin,* 317 U.S. at 19, the *Quirin* Court moved directly to the legal principles applicable to unlawful combatants, and then to the application of those principles to the undisputed facts. Other controlling cases date to World War II, the Civil War, and even further back. . . .

However, if the case law seems sparse and some of the cases abstruse, that is not because courts have not recognized and do not continue to recognize the President's authority to act when it comes to defending this country. Recall that in Zadvydas v. Davis, even as the Supreme Court placed limits on the government's authority to detain immigrants awaiting deportation, 533 U.S. at 691-97, 701, the Court was careful to point out that the case before it did not involve "terrorism or other special circumstances where special arguments might be made for forms of preventive detention and for heightened deference to the judgments of the political branches with respect to matters of national security," *id.* at 696. The "political branches," when they make judgments on the exercise of war powers under Articles I and II, as both branches have here, need not submit those judgments to review by Article III courts. Rather, they are subject to the perhaps less didactic but nonetheless searching audit of the democratic process. . . .

The deference to which the Supreme Court and the Fourth Circuit refer is due not because judges are not personally able to decide whether facts have been established by competent evidence, or whether those facts are sufficient to warrant a particular conclusion by a preponderance of evidence, or by clear and convincing evidence, or beyond a reasonable doubt. Indeed, if there is any task suited to what should be the job skills of judges, deciding such issues is it. Rather, deference is due because of a principle captured in another "statement of Justice Jackson – that we decide difficult cases presented to us by virtue of our commissions, not our competence." Dames & Moore v. Regan, 453 U.S. 654, 661 (1981). That principle applies equally to the case a judge feels unqualified for but must decide, as to the case a judge feels well qualified for but may not decide. The commission of a judge, as *The Prize Cases* and the quoted language from *Zadvydas* suggest, does not run to deciding *de novo* whether Padilla is associated with al Qaeda and whether he should therefore be detained as an unlawful combatant. It runs only to deciding two things: (i) whether the controlling political authority – in this case, the President – was in fact exercising a power vouchsafed to him by the Constitution and the laws; that determination, in turn, is to be made only by examining whether there is some evidence to support his conclusion that Padilla was, like the German saboteurs in *Quirin,* engaged in a mission against the United States on behalf of an enemy with whom the United States is at war, and (ii) whether that evidence has not been entirely mooted by subsequent events. The first determination – that there is some evidence of Padilla's hostile status – would support the President's assertion in the June 9 Order that he was exercising the power referred to above. That is the "some evidence" test suggested in the government's papers, and it will be applied once Padilla presents any facts he may wish to present to the court.

B. *The Sealed Mobbs Declaration*

There remains the question of whether the court will consider the Sealed Mobbs Declaration not only to help decide whether Padilla presents a particular danger if he is allowed to consult with counsel, as has already been done, but also to help decide whether there was some evidence to support the President's decision to designate him an enemy combatant, and whether such evidence has not become moot. Padilla objects to my doing so, arguing that he has a fundamental right to avoid suffering serious injury based on facts that are not disclosed. Thus, he cites Greene v. McElroy, 360 U.S. 474 (1959), where the Supreme Court reversed denial of a security clearance to the employee of a defense contractor based on confidential reports .... Although the government has not discussed *Greene* in its reply papers, the case is distinguishable from this one on several bases, including that the confidential evidence was used before an executive agency and without explicit delegation from Congress or the President. *Id.* at 507. . . .

. . . However, the Sealed Mobbs Declaration does not engage issues of fairness to the extent that might at first be supposed because it does not broaden the nature of the accusations against Padilla beyond the bounds of the Mobbs Declaration itself, nor does it refer to conduct by Padilla that is not described in the Mobbs Declaration. Instead, other than identifying one or more of the sources referred to only in cryptic terms in the Mobbs Declaration, the sealed document simply sets forth objective circumstantial evidence that corroborates the factual allegations in the Mobbs Declaration. Padilla's access to the unclassified Mobbs Declaration gives him all the notice necessary to meet the allegations of whom he had contact with and what he did, or to explain why those allegations are now moot. . . .

. . . If, after Padilla has had an opportunity to contest the unsealed Mobbs Declaration, I find that the government has failed to meet the some evidence standard, I will decide whether to consider the sealed document. At that point, I will have two options: (1) I could find that it is impermissible to use the sealed document without giving Padilla access to it, in which case the government will have the option of withdrawing the submission; or (2) I could consider the sealed document *in camera*. Before Padilla has disputed any facts, it would be premature to choose between these options. . . .

NOTES AND QUESTIONS

1. *Greater Includes the Lesser?* In both *Hamdi* and *Padilla* the courts assume that Supreme Court precedents concerning trial by military commission, especially *Quirin*, are apposite to the legality of military detention. *Quirin* did say that both lawful and unlawful combatants "are subject to capture and detention," and that unlawful combatants are additionally subject to military trial and punishment (casebook p. 895). This the *Padilla* court understood to reflect the Supreme Court's belief that "detention alone . . . [is] certainly the lesser of the consequences an

unlawful combatant could face." 233 F. Supp. 2d at 595. But is that always true? The unlawful combatant who is tried at least will see a resolution of his status. What about the combatant who is detained by the military without trial or even charges indefinitely, or until the political branches determine that the war is over? If detention is not the "lesser" consequence for such a combatant, is case law establishing the legality of a military trial sufficient to establish the legality of detention?

2. *What Kind of War?* Military detention is described as a "war power" by the *Hamdi* court. If authority for such detention presupposes a war, is a state of war sufficient, as the Supreme Court defined that term in *The Prize Cases* (casebook p. 73), or must it be expressly authorized by Congress?

Does 18 U.S.C. §4001(a) bear on this question? In *Padilla*, the government argued that this provision is inapplicable to wartime detentions ordered by the Commander in Chief. Reconsider the history of this statute. *See* casebook at p. 735, Note 6 and p. 53 in this Supplement. Is the government's argument sound?

Both *Hamdi* and *Padilla* ultimately conclude that the post-9/11 authorization for the use of force, in any case, satisfies §4001(a). But should that section be read to require express and specific authorization? *Compare* 18 U.S.C. §4001(a) *with* 18 U.S.C. §1385 (Posse Comitatus Act) (reproduced at casebook p. 766). Does the September 18, 2001, resolution for the use of force apply to uses of force (and, by implication, military detention) *within* the United States, or just in Afghanistan? See Stephen I. Vladeck, *A Small Problem of Precedent: 18 U.S.C. §4001(a) and the Detention of U.S. Citizen "Enemy Combatants,"* 112 Yale L.J. 961, 967 (2003) (arguing that it fails to satisfy §4001(a)). Compare the declaration of war on Germany, which stated that "the President is hereby authorized and directed to employ the entire naval and military forces of the United States and the resources of the Government to carry on war against the Government of Germany." Act of Dec. 11, 1941, ch. 564, 55 Stat. 796.

Suppose Congress had not statutorily authorized the use of force against terrorist organizations like Al Qaeda, but the President had gone ahead anyway on the theory of repelling attack. Would military detention of combatants in that war be authorized? What about persons detained as terrorists generally in an undeclared "war on terrorism"?

3. *Necessity for Military Detention.* The practical necessity for military detention is plain. United States soldiers who take prisoners in the field or encounter suspicious persons have to do something with them, at least until their mission is accomplished or their force secured or both. Bringing such

persons before a judge, or even holding some kind of hearing while the bullets are flying, is out of the question. Moving them back from the front lines is no cure, because it is often still impractical to withdraw troops from the front to give testimony or to preserve evidence during the fighting. The necessity arguments for military trial were implicit in *Milligan* and *Quirin; Hamdi* makes them explicitly. *See also* Odah v. United States, 321 F.3d 1134, 1150 (D.C. Cir. 2003) (Randolph, J., concurring) (asserting with respect to military detainees at Camp X-Ray in Guantanamo Naval Base, Cuba, that "[t]he historical meaning of 'in the field' was not restricted to the field of battle. It applied as well to 'organized camps stationed in remote places where civil courts did not exist'").

If these arguments apply to Hamdi, do they also apply to Padilla? Of course, some of the evidence against him may come from overseas, but that would not differentiate his case from those of many other international criminals who are tried in our courts. On the other hand, Padilla's Mobbs affidavit avers that some of the key evidence against him comes from the interrogation of Al Qaeda operatives detained abroad. If military necessity justifies their detention, does it somehow derivatively justify his as well? If your answer is yes, where is the stopping point? Can the military indefinitely detain any U.S. citizen arrested in the United States for activities planned here as long as any of the evidence against him is derived from persons properly detained abroad, or collected on a battlefield?

How would you reframe the authority for military detention to confine it strictly to situations of military necessity?

4. *Determining Combatant Status.* Recall the differences in the status of Milligan and Quirin. Is Hamdi more like Milligan or like Quirin? What about Padilla? Note that nothing in *Hamdi* or *Padilla* denies that *Milligan* is still good law. If this is true, how would you now differentiate Milligan's status? How would you distinguish *Milligan*?

The *Hamdi* court concludes that no hearing is needed to confirm Hamdi's combatant status because he was concededly captured on the battlefield. Who conceded it? Hamdi has never appeared in court; indeed, the government would presumably decline to produce him. A client's lawyer can make concessions for him, but only when the client has authorized him to do so, which presumably requires them to communicate. Even in Hamdi's case, in other words, there is a logical argument for Hamdi to have access to his lawyer and vice-versa before the court accepts the government's characterizations about Hamdi's status.

Moreover, even if Hamdi was caught carrying an assault rifle on the battlefield in Afghanistan, does this, without more, make him a combatant? Some wags have observed that in Afghanistan *everyone* carries a weapon,

Chapter 13. Consequence Management: When the Worst Happens 87

many of them AK-47s taken from the Russians. Even foreign aid workers are sometimes armed for their own protection.

None of this is to claim that Hamdi is not exactly who Mobbs claims he is, but how can we know without some test of the assertions by a lawyer with access to Hamdi? Such arguments are even stronger, of course, in Padilla's case, because he was picked up at O'Hare Airport in Chicago, not on an Afghan battlefield. Without any concession from Padilla, the issue is how much evidence the government must produce to show that he is a combatant subject to military detention. What standard does the *Padilla* court adopt? Can you propose an alternative?

In late June 2003, President Bush designated a third person as an "enemy combatant." *See* Eric Lichtblau, *Bush Declares Student an Enemy Combatant*, N.Y. Times, June 24, 2003, at A15. Ali Saleh Kahlah al-Marri, a citizen of Qatar, was taken into custody in late 2001 in Peoria, Illinois, as a material witness, then charged with lying to the F.B.I. and credit card fraud and scheduled for trial in a federal court in Illinois. United States v. Al-Marri, Cr. No. 03-10044 (C.D. Ill.). Immediately following his designation as an enemy combatant, al-Marri was, like Hamdi and Padilla, transferred to a military brig in South Carolina. Can you guess why his status was changed after a criminal prosecution was well underway? Do you think his earlier status will affect his treatment as an enemy combatant?

5. *The Right to Assistance of Counsel.* Can any standard for determining Padilla's status work without his input? Can he give that input without a lawyer? Many have argued that the right to assistance of counsel is the most important right of a person detained or prosecuted by the government because it is essential to effectively asserting every other right.

The government responded to such concerns that "[t]he rights the Constitution affords persons in the criminal justice system simply do not apply in the context of detention of enemy combatants." Letter from Daniel J. Bryant (Assistant Attorney General, U.S. Dept. of Justice) to Carl Levin (Chairman of the Senate Committee on Armed Services) (Nov. 26, 2002), at 4. But doesn't this beg the question whether a detainee *is* an "enemy combatant"? Even if military detention and trial operate in some legal universe parallel to the Constitution, does it follow that the President alone is gatekeeper to that universe? If the court has some gatekeeping function as well, how can it fulfill that function without help from the detainee and his counsel?

Consider the following recommendations from the American Bar Association Task Force on Treatment of Enemy Combatants:

RESOLVED, That the American Bar Association urges that U.S. citizens and residents who are detained within the United States based on their designation as "enemy combatants" be afforded the opportunity for meaningful judicial review of their status, under a standard according such deference to the designation as the review court determines to be appropriate to accommodate the needs of the detainee and the requirements of national security; and

FURTHER RESOLVED, That the American Bar Association urges that U.S. citizens and residents who are detained within the United States based on their designations as "enemy combatants" not be denied access to counsel in connection with the opportunity for such review, subject to appropriate conditions as may be set by the court to accommodate the needs of the detainee and the requirements of national security . . . .

American Bar Association, Task Force on Treatment of Enemy Combatants, *Report to the House of Delegates* (2003).

On March 11, 2003, the *Padilla* court emphatically confirmed its earlier order concerning Padilla's right of access to counsel. Padilla v. Rumsfeld, 243 F. Supp. 2d 42 (S.D.N.Y. 2003). It stated that whether or not the government was right in claiming that Padilla's continued isolation was necessary for ongoing interrogation, he has a statutory and constitutional right to present facts to rebut the Mobbs declaration, even under a relaxed "some evidence" standard of proof for the government, and a commensurate right to consult counsel to that end. *Id.* at 54.

6. *Alien Detainees' Access to U.S. Courts.* The public defender who first tried to file a habeas petition on Hamdi's behalf was eventually held to lack standing. Subsequently, Hamdi's father was permitted to petition on his behalf as next friend.

Detainees at Camp X-Ray at the Guantanamo Naval Base in Cuba have fared less well. In Coalition of Clergy v. Bush, 310 F.3d 1153 (9th Cir. 2002), the court found that a group of clergy, lawyers, and professors lacked standing as "next friends" to petition for habeas on the detainees' behalf. In Odah v. United States, 321 F.3d 1134 (D.C. Cir. 2003), the court dismissed habeas petitions filed on behalf of Guantanamo detainees by family members, not on standing grounds, but because the court determined that the detainees – all aliens – had no rights under the Constitution that could be vindicated by the court.

[T]he Guantanamo detainees have much in common with the German prisoners in *Eisentrager*. They too are aliens, they too were captured during military operations, they were in a foreign country when captured, they are now abroad, they are in the custody of the American military, and

Chapter 13. Consequence Management: When the Worst Happens 89

> they have never had any presence in the United States. . . . [W]e believe that under *Eisentrager* these factors preclude the detainees from seeking habeas relief in the courts of the United States. [*Id.* at 1140.]

The court went on to read *Eisentrager* to mean that constitutional rights under the First, Second, Fourth, Fifth, and Sixth Amendments "are not held by aliens outside the sovereign territory of the United States, regardless of whether they are enemy aliens." *Id.* at 1141. Then, drawing upon the Supreme Court's decision in United States v. Verdugo-Urquidez, 494 U.S. 259 (1990) (casebook p. 642), and its own opinion in Harbury v. Deutch, 233 F.3d 596 (D.C. Cir. 2000) (casebook p. 548), the court declared that "non-resident aliens . . . plainly cannot appeal to the protection of the Constitution or laws of the United States." 321 F.3d at 1141.

> The consequence is that no court in this country has jurisdiction to grant habeas relief, under 28 U.S.C. §2241, to the Guantanamo detainees, even if they have not been adjudicated enemies of the United States. We cannot see why, or how, the writ may be made available to aliens abroad when basic constitutional protections are not. This much is at the heart of *Eisentrager*. If the Constitution does not entitle the detainees to due process, and it does not, they cannot invoke the jurisdiction of our courts to test the constitutionality or the legality of restraints on their liberty. [*Id.*]

Finally, the *Odah* court noted that its analysis depended on a finding that the detainees were not "within any territory over which the United States is sovereign," *id.* at 1142, and that as a lessee from the Cuban government, the United States lacks sovereignty over its naval base at Guantanamo.

Can you think of some other way to test the propriety of these detentions? *See generally* John W. Broomes, *Maintaining Honor in Troubled Times: Defining the Rights of Terrorism Suspects Detained in Cuba*, 42 Washburn L.J. 107 (2002); American Bar Association, Task Force on Treatment of Enemy Combatants, *Preliminary Report* (Aug. 8, 2002).

14

Trying International Terrorists

A. CRIMINALIZING SEDITION, TERRORISM, AND SUPPORT FOR TERRORISM

Page 838. Add this material at the end of Note 2.

Regarding the *Rahman* prosecution, *see generally* John Alan Cohen, *Seditious Conspiracy, The Smith Act, and Prosecution for Religious Speech Advocating the Violent Overthrow of Government*, 17 St. John's J. Legal Comment. 199 (2003).

Page 839. Add this material at the end of Note 5.

The statute making material support of terrorist activities a felony, 18 U.S.C. §2339B(a)(1) (discussed in *Reno*), has emerged as the government's weapon of choice against suspected terrorists since 9/11. The threat of a fifteen-year prison term is apparently being wielded as an inducement for defendants to plead out. *See* Siobhan Roth, *Material Support Law: Weapon in War on Terror*, Legal Times, May 5, 2003, at 11.

D. TRYING TERRORISTS AND OTHER INTERNATIONAL CRIMINALS

1. Secret Information in Proceedings Against Terrorists

Page 878. Add this material at the end of Note 3.

The risk of inaccuracy from using secret evidence may also be illustrated by a case described by the Washington Post as "the only criminal case since the Sept. 11 attacks in which secret evidence was presented against the defendant." *See* Dale Russakoff, *N.J. Judge Unseals Transcript in Controversial Terror Case*, Wash. Post, June 25, 2003, at A3. Reportedly local (non-federal) prosecutors convinced a state judge during a bail hearing that evidence against a defendant whom they alleged had ties to terrorists was so sensitive that the defendant could not be allowed to see it. Months later, an appellate judge ruled that prosecutors had not shown the defendant to be a security risk, and the trial judge then unsealed the bail hearing transcript. *Id.*; Robert Hanley & Jonathan Miller, *4 Transcripts Are Released in Case Tied to 9/11 Hijackers*, N.Y. Times, June 25, 2003, at B5; Jennifer V. Hughes, *Supposed Links to Terrorism Revealed,* The Record, June 25, 2003, at A01. Most of the evidence consisted of testimony by a detective about what he had heard from FBI agents about the defendant. Federal authorities, however, contradicted or denied knowledge of some of this information after release of the transcripts, and the defendant's attorney dismissed it as "slanderous, hearsay, double- and triple-hearsay, evidence which he claimed he could have rebutted if only he and the defendant had been allowed to see it." Russakoff, *supra*. "To think that they kept me in jail on this," the defendant said, after being held for six months as a suspected terrorist. *Id.* The state dropped all but one of 25 counts of selling fraudulent documents to Hispanic immigrants (none tied to terrorism).

Page 888. Add this material after Note 8.

NOTE ON UNITED STATES V. MOUSSAOUI

Zacarias Moussaoui, a 35-year-old French citizen of Moroccan descent, is, at this writing, the only person to have been charged in a federal court as a 9/11 conspirator. A resident of the United Kingdom before 2001, Moussaoui is alleged to have attended Al Qaeda training in Afghanistan and Malaysia before traveling to the United States in February 2001 with $35,000 in cash. He attended one flight school in Oklahoma, contacted

Chapter 14. Trying International Terrorists 93

another in Florida, and enrolled in a third school in Minnesota, where his peculiar behavior caused flight instructors to notify the FBI. Government agents arrested him on Aug. 16, 2001, on an immigration violation. The 9/11 attacks occurred while Moussaoui was in federal custody.

Subsequently, Moussaoui was indicted in federal court and charged with multiple counts of conspiracy to commit terrorism, aircraft piracy, murder, and destruction of property. The government also gave notice of intent to seek the death penalty. As the district court described it, "the United States' apparent theory of the case is that Moussaoui was to pilot a fifth hijacked airplane and crash it into the White House." United States v. Moussaoui, Cr. No. 01-455-A, slip op. at 3 (E.D. Va. March 10, 2003) (redacted). Moussaoui readily admitted to being a member of Al Qaeda, but insisted that he was not part of the 9/11 plot and instead part of another operation to occur outside the United States after 9/11 involving different members of Al Qaeda. *Id.*

The indictment prominently linked Moussaoui to one Ramzi Bin al-Shibh. Bin al-Shibh is alleged to have formed an Al Qaeda terrorist cell in Germany, where he shared an apartment with Moussaoui and worked with hijacker Mohammed Atta. United States v. Moussaoui, Cr. No. 01-455-A, Superseding Indictment (E.D. Va. 2002). The indictment alleges that Bin al-Shibh wired money to several of the hijackers in the United States, as well as to Moussaoui in Oklahoma, and that Moussaoui shortly afterwards purchased knives and flight lessons.

After the indictments, Bin al-Shibh was captured in Pakistan and apparently transported to Guantanamo Naval Base, where he is being held in U.S. military detention. Moussaoui then sought to depose Bin al-Shibh. Although redactions in the public filings conceal the details, it appears that Moussaoui sought access to Bin al-Shibh both because he was identified as a co-conspirator in the indictment, and, on *Brady* grounds, to develop exculpatory testimony. *See* United States v. Moussaoui, Cr. No. 01-455-A, slip op. (E.D. Va. March 10, 2003) (redacted for "Top Secret" content); United States v. Moussaoui, No. 03-4162, Brief of the Appellee (4th Cir. April 1, 2003) (redacted). Thus, standby counsel for Moussaoui assert:

> When REDACTED information is viewed in the context of other defense evidence, and indeed in the context of all of the evidence in the case, its significant exculpatory nature as a missing link in the defense chain of circumstantial proof becomes manifest. Namely, that Moussaoui was a problematical and unstable hanger-on who could never be trusted to be a participant in any significant undertaking by al Quaeda and was not a participant in the plan for the September 11 attacks. Were a jury to nevertheless return a verdict of guilty, the REDACTED evidence would become even more significant in the penalty phase, defining Moussaoui's

role as minor and eliminating the Government's ability to prove anything he did caused death. [*Id.* at 35 (redactions in original).]

The government resisted allowing any pretrial access to Bin al-Shibh on the grounds that it would interfere with his interrogation and therefore with military operations to which his intelligence would be vital, and thus "entangle the court in the post hoc micro-management of the conduct of the war." United States v. Moussaoui, Cr. No. 01-455-A, slip op. at 2, 10 (E.D. Va. March 10, 2003) (redacted).

Drawing on the Classified Information Procedures Act as "the most analogous framework with which to resolve" these issues, the trial court first found that the testimony of Bin al-Shibh was relevant to Moussaoui's defense because he might provide material, favorable testimony on Moussaoui's behalf, both as to guilt and as to potential punishment. *Id.* at 16-17. After balancing the government's asserted interest in not interrupting the flow of ongoing intelligence gathering against Moussaoui's due process and Sixth Amendment rights, the court then found that "granting standby counsel unmonitored, pretrial access to REDACTED would implicate too many of the security interests identified by the United States." *Id.* at 24. The court therefore granted access only under several undisclosed but presumably restrictive conditions, before concluding its opinion with the following observation:

> When the Government elected to bring Moussaoui to trial in this civilian tribunal, it assumed the responsibility of abiding by well-established principles of due process. To the extent that the United States seeks a categorical, "wartime" exception to the Sixth Amendment, it should reconsider whether the civilian criminal courts are the appropriate fora in which to prosecute alleged terrorists captured in the context of an ongoing war. [*Id.* at 26.]

The government neither complied with the trial court's access order, nor, apparently, proposed substitutions in accordance with the CIPA scheme, but instead took an interlocutory appeal. Conceding that the "appeal is one of extraordinary importance," the Court of Appeals ruled that the trial court order was not yet appealable because the government had yet to definitively disobey it. United States v. Moussaoui, 2003 WL 21467775 (4th Cir. June 26, 2003).

NOTES AND QUESTIONS

1. *Access by or to Enemy Combatants?* The government has argued that Johnson v. Eisentrager, 339 U.S. 763 (1950) (described at casebook pp.

Chapter 14. Trying International Terrorists 95

644 and 815, Note 6) stands for the proposition that federal courts cannot exercise power over alien enemy combatants abroad, and that the *Moussaoui* court therefore lacks the power to order access to Bin al-Shibh. Reply Brief for the United States at 12-13, United States v. Moussaoui, No. 03-4162 (4th Cir. May 13, 2003) (redacted). In *Eisentrager*, however, it was the alien enemy combatant who sought access to courts for a writ of habeas corpus. Can you distinguish *Eisentrager*? Even if Bin al-Shibh cannot be reached by the federal court, does that mean the government can proceed with its criminal prosecution of Moussaoui if it persists in refusing the requested access?

2. *"Wartime" Exception.* Can you make an argument for a broader "wartime exception" to the Sixth Amendment that does not depend in any way on Bin al-Shibh's location? Consider whether *Keith* (casebook p. 615), *Korematsu* (casebook p. 796), or *Zadvydas* (casebook p. 732, Note 1) might be relevant.

3. *CIPA by Analogy.* The district court looked to CIPA for "the most analogous framework" for analysis. Why did CIPA not directly control? By what authority did the trial court undertake the relevance and balancing inquiries, and order conditional access? Did the court, in effect, create a "wartime exception" to the Sixth Amendment after all?

4. *Switching Fora?* The district court invited the government to "reconsider whether the civilian criminal courts are the appropriate fora" for trying someone like Moussaoui. The alternative is trial by military commission, which we explore at casebook pp. 889-906. Indeed, even Moussaoui's standby counsel appears to have invited this alternative, gratuitously conceding that the government's authority to try enemy combatants by military commission is "settled," and implying that the government can simply dismiss the criminal prosecution and proceed instead by a military commission to resolve the tension between Moussaoui's Sixth Amendment rights and the war powers. Brief of the Appellee at 3-4, United States v. Moussaoui, No. 03-4162 (4th Cir. May 13, 2003).

After you read the materials on military commissions, you can decide for yourself whether this is a wise concession. But do you agree with the apparent assumption upon which it and the district court's invitation rest – that the government can switch fora in midstream? Even assuming that the government could lawfully have tried Moussaoui by military commission *ab initio*, does it necessarily follow that it can start in a civilian court and then dismiss in favor of a military commission when it is unhappy with the civilian court's rulings? Would it matter how far the criminal prosecution had progressed beyond the indictment? If such a switch survived constitutional challenges, would it nevertheless violate the spirit of the law?

Page 903. Add this material after Note 4.

On April 30, 2003, the Department of Defense issued an instruction defining crimes that could be tried by military commissions. The instruction purports to be "declarative of existing law" of armed conflict. Most of the listed crimes require a nexus with armed conflict – "in the context of and . . . associated with armed conflict" – which nevertheless

> does not require a declaration of war, ongoing mutual hostilities, or confrontation involving a regular national armed force. A single hostile act or attempted act may provide sufficient basis for the nexus so long as its magnitude or severity rises to the level of an "armed attack" or an "act of war," or the number, power, stated intent or organization of the force with which the actor is associated is such that the act or attempted act is tantamount to an attack by an armed force. [Department of Defense, Military Commission Instruction No. 2, at §5(C) (April 30, 2003).]

The instruction includes commonly recognized war crimes, such as willful killing of protected persons and attacking civilians, civilian objects, or protected property, as well as other offenses such as hijacking, terrorism, murder by an unprivileged belligerent, and aiding the enemy. "Terrorism" is defined as intentionally killing or harming one or more persons or engaging in an act that is inherently dangerous to another and evinces a wanton disregard of human life, to intimidate or coerce a civilian population, or to influence the policy of a government by intimidation or coercion, "in the context of and was associated with armed conflict." *Id*. §6(B)(2). Aiding and abetting, soliciting, conspiring to commit, or being an accessory after the fact to terrorism are also defined as crimes. Comments to the instructions state that solicitation of terrorism "may be by means other than speech and writing. Any act or conduct that reasonably may be construed as a serious request, order, inducement, advice, or offer of assistance to commit any offense triable by military commission may constitute solicitation." *Id*. at §6(C)(2)(b)(2). Do these instructions resolve the questions raised in Note 4? *If* the Constitution applies to prosecutions brought before military commissions, do you see any constitutional problems raised by the substantive offenses defined in the instructions?

Chapter 14. Trying International Terrorists

Page 906. Add these materials after Note 6.

The final procedures have been issued and are consistent with the Note's account of the draft procedures. Department of Defense, Military Commission Order No. 1 (March 21, 2002). A more recent instruction, however, has caused its own controversy. *See* Office of the Secretary, Department of Defense, *Qualification of Civilian Defense Counsel*, 68 Fed. Reg. 39391 (proposed July 1, 2003) (to be codified at 32 C.F.R. pt. 14). This instruction requires such counsel to take an oath that:

> I will not travel or transmit documents from the site of the proceedings without the approval of the Appointing Authority or the Presiding Officer. The Defense Team and I will otherwise perform all of our work relating to the proceedings, including any electronic or other research, at the site of the proceedings . . . .
>
> I will not discuss or otherwise communicate or share documents or information about the case with anyone except persons who have been designated as members of the Defense Team . . . .
>
> I understand that my communications with my client, even if traditionally covered by the attorney-client privilege, may be subject to monitoring or review by government officials, using any available means, for security and intelligence purposes. I understand that any such monitoring will only take place in limited circumstances when approved by proper authority, and that any evidence or information derived from such communications will not be used in proceedings against the Accused who made or received the relevant communication. . . . [*Id.* Annex B, ¶¶II(E)(1), (2), and (I).]

What issues, if any, do these requirements present for civilian lawyers subject to the Model Rules of Professional Responsibility? "An attorney would be committing malpractice by signing their affidavit," one lawyer is reported as asserting. *See* Vanessa Blum, *The Outlines of Justice*, Legal Times, May 26, 2003, at 1. Reportedly, the promulgation of these requirements has discouraged civilian lawyers from applying. "Who's going to want to take a case where your conversations are going to be overheard, you are not going to be able to speak about the case to the press or anyone else, you are not going to be able to see classified evidence that's being used to convict your client, and your case is going to essentially take over your life – often without compensation?" asks one law professor and veteran lawyer for immigrant terrorist suspects. *See* Dan Christensen, *Veteran Attorneys Blast Rules for Military Trials*, Legal Intelligencer, May 15, 2003, at 4. "[T]he only thing more difficult than getting out of Guantanamo may be finding a lawyer willing to participate as civilian defense counsel in a military tribunal." David Cole, *Defending Show Trials*, The Nation, June 15, 2003, at 6. In response to these comments, the Defense Department is reportedly considering changing its requirements.

Recall, on the other hand, that the military lawyers on the defense team have access to all proceedings and evidence. Does this compensate for the restrictions on civilian defense counsel? Do you think that it is accurate to call the anticipated military trials "show trials" or "kangaroo courts"? Are there less restrictive ways to address legitimate government interests in security during the trials?

7. *Detainees Designated for Trial.* On July 3, 2003, President Bush designated six individuals as eligible for trial by military commission, pursuant to his November 13, 2001, Military Order. *See* Neil A. Lewis, *Six Detainees May Soon Face Military Trials,* N.Y. Times, July 4, 2003, at A1. Neither their identities nor reasons for their designation were immediately revealed, but they are reportedly likely to be tried in a secure courtroom at the Guantanamo Naval Base.

15

Public Access to National Security Information

A. EXECUTIVE ORDER NO. 12,958 – CLASSIFIED NATIONAL SECURITY INFORMATION

Page 923. Add this material after Note 7.

8. *Readjusting the Balance: A New Executive Order.* On March 25, 2003, President Bush signed a new executive order on classification amending, rather than replacing, the 1995 Clinton order. Exec. Order No. 13,292, 68 Fed. Reg. 15, 315 (2003). The new order renumbers many sections and includes a variety of important substantive changes. Among them, the categories of information that may be classified have been increased to include "transnational terrorism," §§1.1(a)(4), 1.4(e), "vulnerabilities or capabilities of... infrastructures," §1.4(f), and "weapons of mass destruction." §1.4(h). No definitions are provided for any of these terms. In addition, information that has been declassified now may be reclassified under certain conditions. §1.7(c).

Significantly, the new order preserves the requirement of a determination that "the unauthorized disclosure of the information reasonably could be expected to result in damage to the national security ... and the original classification authority is able to identify or describe the damage." §1.1(4). On the other hand, the presumption against classification in §1.2(b) of the earlier order has been removed. And the new order provides that the "unauthorized disclosure of foreign government information is presumed to cause damage to the national security." §1.1(c).

100   Chapter 15. Public Access to National Security Information

How do you think these changes might affect agency practice in classifying records or the response of courts to FOIA suits challenging that practice?

B. THE FREEDOM OF INFORMATION ACT

1. The Statutory Text

Page 930. Add this material at the end of Note 4.

Until 2002, FOIA could be utilized by "any person" to obtain agency records. The Intelligence Authorization Act for FY 2003, however, amended 5 U.S.C. §552(a)(3) to bar requests from foreign governments, international governmental organizations, or their representatives for records held by elements of the intelligence community. Pub. L. No. 107-306, §312, 116 Stat. 2383, 2390-2391 (2002). *See* U.S. Department of Justice, *FOIA Amended by Intelligence Authorization Act,* FOIA Post, Dec. 23, 2002, *at http://www.usdoj.gov/oip/foiapost/2002foiapost38.htm.* This change was reportedly intended to prevent access to intelligence agency records by states that support terrorism. See H.R. Rep. No. 107-592, at 27 (2002). Can you think of any other reasons to adopt such a restriction?

2. Statutory Exemptions and Judicial Review

Page 946. Add this material at the end of Note 7.

In recent years, business groups have argued that if companies learned of a security problem in their information systems, they were reluctant to forward the information to federal officials because they feared the information could later be accessed under FOIA. In response to these concerns, §214 of the Homeland Security Act amended FOIA to exempt from disclosure "critical infrastructure information" that is "voluntarily" submitted to the federal government. Homeland Security Act of 2002, Pub. L. No. 107-296, §214, 116 Stat. 2135, 2151. The Act also bars the government from using any such submitted information "in any civil action arising under Federal or State law." *Id.* §214(a)(1)(c). Billed as an important component of information sharing after the September 11 attacks, the new FOIA exemption prompted opponents to argue that the provision permits companies to submit broad categories of information to the government, including company misdeeds, and deny any other agency or person access to the information. *See Homeland Security Act Will Affect*

Chapter 15. Public Access to National Security Information 101

Individual Privacy, Experts Say, 71 U.S.L.W. 2387-2388 (Dec. 17, 2002). Can you articulate the two sides in this debate? Can you see the potential for abuse of the new exemption?

The Homeland Security Act also directed the President to develop procedures to "identify and safeguard homeland security information that is sensitive but unclassified." Pub. L. No. 107-296, §892(a)(1)(B), 116 Stat. 2135, 2253. Congress neglected, however, to define the term "sensitive" or to indicate how access to such information might be restricted. *See* Geneviev Knezo, *"Sensitive but Unclassified" and Other Federal Security Controls on Scientific and Technical Information: History and Current Controversy* (Cong. Res. Serv. 2003).

Page 948. Add this material at the end of Note 9.

Center for National Security Studies v. United States Department of Justice

United States Court of Appeals, District of Columbia Circuit, 2003
331 F.3d 918

SENTELLE, Circuit Judge: Various "public interest" groups (plaintiffs) brought this Freedom of Information Act (FOIA) action against the Department of Justice (DOJ or government) seeking release of information concerning persons detained in the wake of the September 11 terrorist attacks, including: their names, their attorneys, dates of arrest and release, locations of arrest and detention, and reasons for detention. . . . The district court ordered release of the names of the detainees and their attorneys, but held that the government could withhold all other detention information pursuant to FOIA Exemption 7(A). . . . Upon *de novo* review, we agree with the district court that the detention information is properly covered by Exemption 7(A); but we further hold that Exemption 7(A) justifies withholding the names of the detainees and their attorneys. We also reject plaintiffs' alternate theories that the First Amendment and the common law mandate disclosure of the contested information. [Common law and First Amendment-based rights of access to government information are addressed at casebook pp. 957-970 and corresponding portions of this Supplement.] We therefore affirm in part, reverse in part, and remand the case to the district court for the entry of a judgment of dismissal.

Chapter 15. Public Access to National Security Information

I. Background

A. The Investigation

. . . In the course of the post-September 11 investigation, the government interviewed over one thousand individuals about whom concern had arisen. The concerns related to some of these individuals were resolved by the interviews, and no further action was taken with respect to them. Other interviews resulted in the interviewees being detained. As relevant here, these detainees fall into three general categories.

The first category of detainees consists of individuals who were questioned in the course of the investigation and detained by the INS for violation of the immigration laws (INS detainees). INS detainees were initially questioned because there were "indications that they might have connections with, or possess information pertaining to, terrorist activity against the United States including particularly the September 11 attacks and/or the individuals or organizations who perpetrated them." Based on the initial questioning, each INS detainee was determined to have violated immigration law; some of the INS detainees were also determined to "have links to other facets of the investigation." Over 700 individuals were detained on INS charges. As of June 13, 2002, only seventy-four remained in custody. Many have been deported. INS detainees have had access to counsel, and the INS has provided detainees with lists of attorneys willing to represent them, as required by 8 U.S.C. §1229(b)(2) (2000). INS detainees have had access to the courts to file *habeas corpus* petitions. They have also been free to disclose their names to the public.

The second category of detainees consists of individuals held on federal criminal charges (criminal detainees). The government asserts that none of these detainees can be eliminated as a source of probative information until after the investigation is completed. According to the most recent information released by the Department of Justice, 134 individuals have been detained on federal criminal charges in the post-September 11 investigation; 99 of these have been found guilty either through pleas or trials. While many of the crimes bear no direct connection to terrorism, several criminal detainees have been charged with terrorism-related crimes, and many others have been charged with visa or passport forgery, perjury, identification fraud, and illegal possession of weapons. Zacarias Moussaoui, presently on trial for participating in the September 11 attacks, is among those who were detained on criminal charges.

The third category consists of persons detained after a judge issued a material witness warrant to secure their testimony before a grand jury, pursuant to the material witness statute, 18 U.S.C. §3144 (2000) (material witness detainees). Each material witness detainee was believed to have information material to the events of September 11. The district courts before which these material witnesses have appeared have issued sealing orders that prohibit the government from releasing any information about the proceedings. The government has not revealed how many individuals were detained on material witness warrants. At least two individuals initially held as material witnesses are now being held for alleged terrorist activity.

. . . [E]ach of the detainees has had access to counsel, access to the courts, and freedom to contact the press or the public at large.

B. The Litigation

On October 29, 2001, plaintiffs submitted a FOIA request to the Department of Justice seeking . . . information about each detainee [as noted above]. . . .

In response to plaintiffs' FOIA request, the government released some information, but withheld much of the information requested. As to INS detainees, the government withheld the detainees' names, locations of arrest and detention, the dates of release, and the names of lawyers. As to criminal detainees, the government withheld the dates and locations of arrest and detention, the dates of release, and the citizenship status of each detainee. The government withheld all requested information with respect to material witnesses. Although the government has refused to disclose a comprehensive list of detainees' names and other detention information sought by plaintiffs, the government has from time to time publicly revealed names and information of the type sought by plaintiffs regarding a few individual detainees, particularly those found to have some connection to terrorism.

On December 5, 2001, plaintiffs filed this action in district court seeking to compel release of the withheld information pursuant to the Freedom of Information Act, 5 U.S.C. §552. . . .

II. The FOIA Claims . . .

A. Names of Detainees

. . . Upon review, we hold that Exemption 7(A) was properly invoked to withhold the names of the detainees and their lawyers. Finding the names protected under 7(A), we need not address the other exemptions invoked by the government and reserve judgment on whether they too would support withholding the names. . . .

The threshold question here is whether the names of detainees were "compiled for law enforcement purposes." Because the DOJ is an agency "specializ[ing] in law enforcement," its claim of a law enforcement purpose is entitled to deference. Campbell v. Dep't of Justice, 164 F.3d 20, 32 (D.C. Cir. 1998). To establish a law enforcement purpose, DOJ's declarations must establish (1) "a rational nexus between the investigation and one of the agency's law enforcement duties;" and (2) "a connection between an individual or incident and a possible security risk or violation of federal law." *Campbell*, 164 F.3d at 32. The government's proffer easily meets this standard. The terrorism investigation is one of DOJ's chief "law enforcement duties" at this time, and the investigation concerns a heinous violation of federal law as well as a breach of this nation's security. Moreover, the names of the detainees and their connection to the investigation came to the government's attention as a result of that law enforcement investigation.

Nonetheless, plaintiffs contend that detainees' names fall outside Exemption 7 because the names are contained in arrest warrants, INS charging documents, and jail records. Since these documents have traditionally been public, plaintiffs contend, Exemption 7 should not be construed to allow withholding of the names. We disagree. Plaintiffs are seeking a comprehensive listing of individuals detained during the post-September 11 investigation. The names have been compiled for the "law enforcement purpose" of successfully prosecuting the terrorism investigation. As compiled, they constitute a comprehensive diagram of the law enforcement investigation after September 11. Clearly this is information compiled for law enforcement purposes.

Next, plaintiffs urge that Exemption 7(A) does not apply because disclosure is not "reasonably likely to interfere with enforcement proceedings." We disagree. Under Exemption 7(A), the government has the burden of demonstrating a reasonable likelihood of interference with the terrorism investigation. The government's declarations, viewed in light of the appropriate deference to the executive on issues of national security, satisfy this burden.

It is well-established that a court may rely on government affidavits to support the withholding of documents under FOIA exemptions, and that we review the government's justifications therein *de novo*, 5 U.S.C. §552(a)(4)(B). It is equally well-established that the judiciary owes some measure of deference to the executive in cases implicating national security, a uniquely executive purview. *See, e.g.,* Zadvydas v. Davis, 533 U.S. 678, 696 (2001) (noting that "terrorism or other special circumstances" might warrant "heightened deference to the judgments of the political branches"); Dep't of the Navy v. Egan, 484 U.S. 518, 530 (1988) ("courts traditionally

Chapter 15. Public Access to National Security Information

have been reluctant to intrude upon the authority of the executive in military and national security affairs"). Indeed, both the Supreme Court and this Court have expressly recognized the propriety of deference to the executive in the context of FOIA claims which implicate national security. . . .

The need for deference in this case is just as strong as in earlier cases. America faces an enemy just as real as its former Cold War foes, with capabilities beyond the capacity of the judiciary to explore. Exemption 7(A) explicitly requires a predictive judgment of the harm that will result from disclosure of information, permitting withholding when it "could reasonably be expected" that the harm will result. It is abundantly clear that the government's top counterterrorism officials are well-suited to make this predictive judgment. Conversely, the judiciary is in an extremely poor position to second-guess the executive's judgment in this area of national security. We therefore reject any attempt to artificially limit the long-recognized deference to the executive on national security issues. Judicial deference depends on the substance of the danger posed by disclosure – that is, harm to the national security – not the FOIA exemption invoked.

In light of the deference mandated by the separation of powers and Supreme Court precedent, we hold that the government's expectation that disclosure of the detainees' names would enable al Qaeda or other terrorist groups to map the course of the investigation and thus develop the means to impede it is reasonable. A complete list of names informing terrorists of every suspect detained by the government at any point during the September 11 investigation would give terrorist organizations a composite picture of the government investigation, and since these organizations would generally know the activities and locations of its members on or about September 11, disclosure would inform terrorists of both the substantive and geographic focus of the investigation. Moreover, disclosure would inform terrorists which of their members were compromised by the investigation, and which were not. This information could allow terrorists to better evade the ongoing investigation and more easily formulate or revise counter-efforts. In short, the "records could reveal much about the focus and scope of the [agency's] investigation, and are thus precisely the sort of information exemption 7(A) allows an agency to keep secret." Swan v. SEC, 96 F.3d 498, 500 (D.C. Cir. 1996). . . .

Similarly, the government's judgment that disclosure would deter or hinder cooperation by detainees is reasonable. The government reasonably predicts that if terrorists learn one of their members has been detained, they would attempt to deter any further cooperation by that member through intimidation, physical coercion, or by cutting off all contact with the detainee. A terrorist organization may even seek to hunt down detainees (or their families) who are not members of the organization, but who the terrorists know may have valuable information about the organization. . . .

More importantly, some detainees may not be members of terrorist organizations, but may nonetheless have been detained on INS or material witness warrants as having information about terrorists. Terrorist organizations are less likely to be aware of such individuals' status as detainees. Such detainees could be acquaintances of the September 11 terrorists, or members of the same community groups or mosques. These detainees, fearing retribution or stigma, would be less likely to cooperate with the investigation if their names are disclosed. Moreover, tracking down the background and location of these detainees could give terrorists insights into the investigation they would otherwise be unlikely to have. After disclosure, terrorist organizations could attempt to intimidate these detainees or their families, or feed the detainees false or misleading information. It is important to remember that many of these detainees have been released at this time and are thus especially vulnerable to intimidation or coercion. While the detainees have been free to disclose their names to the press or public, it is telling that so few have come forward, perhaps for fear of this very intimidation.

We further note the impact disclosure could have on the government's investigation going forward. A potential witness or informant may be much less likely to come forward and cooperate with the investigation if he believes his name will be made public.

Plaintiffs next argue that the government's predictive judgment is undermined by the government's disclosure of some of the detainees' names. The Supreme Court confronted a similar argument in [CIA v. Sims, 471 U.S. 159 (1985) (noted at casebook p. 944)] in which respondents contended that "because the Agency has already revealed the names of many of the institutions at which [behavior modification] research was performed, the Agency is somehow estopped from withholding the names of others." 471 U.S. at 180. In rejecting the argument, the Court stated that "[t]his suggestion overlooks the political realities of intelligence operations in which, among other things, our Government may choose to release information deliberately to 'send a message' to allies or adversaries." *Id*. We likewise reject the plaintiffs' version of this discredited argument. The disclosure of a few pieces of information in no way lessens the government's argument that complete disclosure would provide a composite picture of its investigation and have negative effects on the investigation. Furthermore, as the *Sims* Court recognized, strategic disclosures can be important weapons in the government's arsenal during a law enforcement investigation. *Id*. The court should not second-guess the executive's judgment in this area. . . .

Contrary to plaintiffs' claims, the government's submissions easily establish an adequate connection between both the material witness and the INS detainees and terrorism to warrant full application of the deference principle. First, all material witness detainees have been held on warrants issued by a federal judge pursuant to 18 U.S.C. §3144. Under this statute, a federal judge may issue a material witness warrant based on an affidavit stating that the witness has information relevant to an ongoing criminal investigation. Consequently, material witness detainees have been found by a federal judge to have relevant knowledge about the terrorism investigation. It is therefore reasonable to assume that disclosure of their names could impede the government's use of these potentially valuable witnesses.

As to the INS detainees, the government states that they were originally questioned because there were indications that they might have connections with, or possess information pertaining to, terrorist activity against the United States including particularly the September 11 attacks and/or the individuals and organizations who perpetrated them. For example, they may have been questioned because they were identified as having interacted with the hijackers, or were believed to have information relating to other aspects of the investigation. . . .

. . . The clear import of the declarations is that many of the detainees have links to terrorism. This comes as no surprise given that the detainees were apprehended during the course of a terrorism investigation, and given that several detainees have been charged with federal terrorism crimes or held as enemy combatants. Accordingly, we conclude that the evidence presented in the declarations is sufficient to show a rational link between disclosure and the harms alleged.

In support of this conclusion, we note that the Third Circuit confronted a similar issue involving the INS detainees when it considered the constitutionality of closed deportation hearings in North Jersey Media Group, Inc. v. Ashcroft, 308 F.3d 198 (3d Cir. 2002), *cert. denied*, 123 S. Ct. 2215 (2003) [Supplement p. 134, *infra*]. The court was faced with the same Watson Declaration in evidence here and the same government prediction that harm would result from the disclosure of information about the INS detainees. That court acknowledged that the "representations of the Watson Declaration are to some degree speculative." *Id.* at 219. But the court did not search for specific evidence that each of the INS detainees was involved in terrorism, nor did it embark on a probing analysis of whether the government's concerns were well-founded. . . . We think the Third Circuit's approach was correct and we follow it here. Inasmuch as the concerns expressed in the government's declarations seem credible – and inasmuch as the declarations were made by counterterrorism experts with far greater knowledge than this Court — we hold that the disclosure of the names of the detainees could reasonably be expected to interfere with the ongoing investigation.

In upholding the government's invocation of Exemption 7(A), we observe that we are in accord with several federal courts that have wisely respected the executive's judgment in prosecuting the national response to terrorism. *See* Hamdi v. Rumsfeld, 316 F.3d 450 (4th Cir. 2003) (dismissing the *habeas corpus* petition of a United States citizen captured in Afghanistan challenging his military detention and designation as an enemy combatant); Global Relief Found. v. O'Neill, 315 F.3d 748 (7th Cir. 2002) (upholding against constitutional challenge a portion of the USA PATRIOT Act, 50 U.S.C. §1702(c), which authorizes the *ex parte* use of classified evidence in proceedings to freeze the assets of terrorist organizations); *North Jersey Media Group*, 308 F.3d 198 (holding that closure of "special interest" deportation hearings involving INS detainees with alleged connections to terrorism does not violate the First Amendment); Hamdi v. Rumsfeld, 296 F.3d 278 (4th Cir. 2002) (reversing district court's order that allowed alleged enemy combatant unmonitored access to counsel). We realize that not all courts are in agreement. In Detroit Free Press v. Ashcroft, 303 F.3d 681 (6th Cir. 2002), the Sixth Circuit acknowledged the necessity of deferring to the executive on terrorism issues but held that the First Amendment prohibits a blanket closure of "special interest deportation hearings." We do not find the Sixth Circuit's reasoning compelling, but join the Third, Fourth, and Seventh Circuits in holding that the courts must defer to the executive on decisions of national security. In so deferring, we do not abdicate the role of the judiciary. Rather, in undertaking a deferential review we simply recognize the different roles underlying the constitutional separation of powers. It is within the role of the executive to acquire and exercise the expertise of protecting national security. It is not within the role of the courts to second-guess executive judgments made in furtherance of that branch's proper role. The judgment of the district court ordering the government to disclose the names of the detainees is reversed.

B. Identity of Counsel

. . . The government contends that a list of attorneys for the detainees would facilitate the easy compilation of a list of all detainees, and all of the dangers flowing therefrom. It is more than reasonable to assume that plaintiffs and *amici* press organizations would attempt to contact detainees' attorneys and compile a list of all detainees. As discussed above, if such a list fell into the hands of al Qaeda, the consequences could be disastrous.

Having accepted the government's predictive judgments about the dangers of disclosing a comprehensive list of detainees, we also defer to its prediction that disclosure of attorneys' names involves the same danger. . . .

C. Other Detention Information

Having held that the government properly withheld the names of the detainees pursuant to Exemption 7(A), we easily affirm the portion of the district court's ruling that allowed withholding, under Exemption 7(A), of the more comprehensive detention information sought by plaintiffs. . . .

IV. Conclusion

For the reasons set forth above, we conclude that the government was entitled to withhold under FOIA Exemption 7(A) the names of INS detainees and those detained as material witnesses in the course of the post-September 11 terrorism investigation; the dates and locations of arrest, detention, and release of all detainees, including those charged with federal crimes; and the names of counsel for detainees. Finally, neither the First Amendment nor federal common law requires the government to disclose the information sought by plaintiffs.

Affirmed in part, reversed in part, and remanded.

TATEL, Circuit Judge, dissenting. . . .

I.

. . . [N]o one can doubt that uniquely compelling governmental interests are at stake: the government's need to respond to the September 11 attacks – unquestionably the worst ever acts of terrorism on American soil – and its ability to defend the nation against future acts of terrorism. But although this court overlooks it, there is another compelling interest at stake in this case: the public's interest in knowing whether the government, in responding to the attacks, is violating the constitutional rights of the hundreds of persons whom it has detained in connection with its terrorism investigation – by, as the plaintiffs allege, detaining them mainly because of their religion or ethnicity, holding them in custody for extended periods without charge, or preventing them from seeking or communicating with legal counsel. The government claims that the detainees have access to counsel and freedom to contact whomever they wish, but the public has a fundamental interest in being able to examine the veracity of such claims.

Just as the government has a compelling interest in ensuring citizens' safety, so do citizens have a compelling interest in ensuring that their government does not, in discharging its duties, abuse one of its most awesome powers, the power to arrest and jail.

Second, while the governmental interests in this case may be uniquely compelling, the legal principles that govern its resolution are not at all unique. The court's opinion emphasizes the national-security implications of the September 11 investigation, but as the government conceded at oral argument, this case is not just about September 11. The law that governs this case is the same law that applies whenever the government's need for confidentiality in a law enforcement investigation runs up against the public's right to know "what [its] government is up to." United States Dep't of Justice v. Reporters Comm. for Freedom of the Press, 489 U.S. 749, 773 (1989). In all such situations, FOIA fully accommodates the government's concerns about the harms that might arise from the release of information pertaining to its investigations. To be sure, the statute strongly favors openness, since Congress recognized that an informed citizenry is "vital to the functioning of a democratic society, needed to check against corruption and to hold the governors accountable to the governed." NLRB v. Robbins Tire & Rubber Co., 437 U.S. 214, 242 (1978). But Congress also recognized that "legitimate governmental and private interests could be harmed by release of certain types of information." John Doe Agency v. John Doe Corp., 493 U.S. 146, 152 (1989). It therefore "provided . . . specific exemptions under which disclosure could be refused," including the four exemptions relevant to this case. . . .

Invoking the "heightened deference to the judgments of the political branches with respect to matters of national security," Zadvydas v. Davis, 533 U.S. 678, 696 (2001), the government refuses to identify the specific categories of information that would actually interfere with its investigation, but rather asks us simply to trust its judgment. This court obeys, declaring that "the judiciary is in an extremely poor position to second-guess the executive's judgment in this area of national security." But requiring agencies to make the detailed showing FOIA requires is not second-guessing their judgment about matters within their expertise. And in any event, this court is also in an extremely poor position to second-guess the legislature's judgment that the judiciary must play a meaningful role in reviewing FOIA exemption requests. Neither FOIA itself nor this circuit's interpretation of the statute authorizes the court to invoke the phrase "national security" to relieve the government of its burden of justifying its refusal to release information under FOIA.

. . . I think it not at all obvious that we owe heightened deference to the government in this case. Citing the legislative history of the 1974

Chapter 15. Public Access to National Security Information 111

amendments to FOIA's Exemption 1, the exemption for national-security matters, we have held that in evaluating Exemption 1 claims, " 'substantial weight' is to be accorded to detailed agency affidavits setting forth the basis for exemption." Weissman v. CIA, 565 F.2d 692, 697 n. 10 (D.C. Cir. 1977).... The government, however, relies on neither Exemption 1 nor the National Security Act in this case, and contrary to the court's suggestion, we have never held that such heightened deference is also appropriate in Exemption 7 cases. Indeed, in *Weissman,* which the court cites for the proposition that "we owe the same deference under Exemption 7(A) in appropriate cases," we found Exemption 7 inapplicable in the case of the CIA's investigation into the FOIA requester's background "except under special collateral circumstances," for instance, to protect the identities of FBI personnel named in requested materials. We instead focused on the deference owed the agency under Exemption 1, as well as Exemption 3 as it incorporates the National Security Act.

In any event, the government's case fails even under the heightened deference we have applied in Exemption 1 and National Security Act cases. No matter the level of deference, our review is not "vacuous." Pratt v. Webster, 673 F.2d 408, 421 (D.C. Cir. 1982)....

II.

... Although I have no doubt that some of the requested information is exempt from FOIA's mandatory disclosure requirement, the court treats disclosure as an all-or-nothing proposition, repeatedly emphasizing the breadth of the plaintiffs' request – the fact that they seek the names and other information pertaining to "every single individual detained in the course of the government's terrorism investigation," as a justification for accepting the government's own very broad, categorical refusal to release the bulk of the requested information. This all-or-nothing approach runs directly counter to well-established principles governing FOIA requests. Nothing in the statute requires requesters to seek only information not exempt from disclosure. To the contrary, the government bears the burden of reviewing the plaintiffs' request, identifying functional categories of information that are exempt from disclosure, and disclosing any reasonably segregable, non-exempt portion of the requested materials. The government fails to satisfy that burden in this case, for the range of circumstances included in the government's exemption request do not "characteristically support" an inference that the information would interfere with its terrorism investigation.

In support of its exemption request, the government offers declarations from two senior officials with responsibility for the terrorism investigation.

One of those declarations, by Dale L. Watson, a Federal Bureau of Investigation official charged with supervising the investigation, was prepared not for this case, but for cases involving the closure of deportation hearings. Watson's declaration thus speaks not to the harm that would flow from disclosing detainees' names or other information, but instead to the harm that would flow from publicly airing evidence about particular detainees at such a hearing .... The court nevertheless relies on the Watson declaration, as well as *North Jersey Media Group*, despite the fact that neither has anything to do with the release of detainee names.

The other declaration, by Department of Justice Terrorism and Violent Crime Section chief James S. Reynolds, does in fact outline the harms that might result from release of some detainee names. But it does not support the government's request for a 7(A) exemption, since that request treats all detainees the same, even though Reynolds tells us that the only common thread among the detainees is that they were "originally questioned because there were indications that they might have connections with, or possess information pertaining to, terrorist activity against the United States." Reynolds Decl. ¶10; *see also id.* ¶¶27, 36. As Reynolds himself acknowledges, this group includes some detainees who have turned out to be innocent of any involvement with terrorist activity and have "no information useful to the investigation." *Id.* ¶36.

Ignoring this important concession, the court declares that "[t]he clear import of the declarations is that many of the detainees have links to terrorism" – which the court considers "no surprise given that the detainees were apprehended during the course of a terrorism investigation, and given that several detainees have been charged with federal terrorism crimes or held as enemy combatants." The court's approach is unconvincing for two reasons.

To begin with, it rests on what seems to be a faulty assumption about facts not in evidence. As of November 5, 2001, the last time the government released a tally, there were 1,182 detainees. Nothing in the record tells us how many of those 1,182 detainees have been charged with federal terrorism crimes or held as enemy combatants. What little information the record does contain, however, suggests that the number may be relatively small. A list of federally charged detainees attached to the government's motion for summary judgment reports that as of the time this suit was filed, only one detainee had been criminally charged in the September 11 attacks and only 108 detainees had been charged with any federal crime – primarily violations of antifraud statutes. Reynolds Decl. ¶27. ...

The only argument that could conceivably support withholding innocent detainees' names is the assertion that disclosure of the names "*may* reveal details about the focus and scope of the investigation and thereby allow terrorists to counteract it." Reynolds Decl. ¶16 (emphasis added). That Reynolds believes these harms *may* result from disclosure is hardly surprising – anything is possible. But before accepting the government's argument, this court must insist on knowing whether these harms "*could reasonably be expected to*" result from disclosure – the standard Congress prescribed for exemption under 7(A). Nothing in Reynolds's declaration suggests that these harms are in fact reasonably likely to occur. . . .

The government's allegations of harm are also undercut by the fact that it has itself provided several other means by which this information can become public. Not only do detainees remain free to inform whomever they choose of their detention, Reynolds Decl. ¶23, but on numerous occasions since September 11, the government itself has disclosed precisely the kind of information it now refuses to provide under FOIA. . . .

IV.

No part of the government's exemption request better illustrates its infirmities than its refusal to disclose the names of the detainees' attorneys. Essentially rehashing its arguments for withholding the names of the attorneys' clients, the government argues – and the court agrees, that releasing attorneys' names would interfere with the terrorism investigation and would compromise the detainees' privacy interests, since releasing a list of attorneys "may facilitate the identification of the detainees themselves." Reynolds Decl. ¶18. The government also claims to be withholding the attorneys' names for their own good, warning that attorneys identified as representing individuals detained in connection with the terrorism investigation "run the risk that they will be subjected to harassment or retaliation in their personal as well as professional lives." Reynolds Decl. ¶26.

Both parts of this argument are not only profoundly wrong, but also reflect a complete misunderstanding of the nature of this country's legal profession. In the first place, attorneys' names are quite clearly not a proxy for the names of their clients. Indeed, recognizing that knowledge of the lawyer's identity does not inexorably lead to identifying the client, ethical rules forbid lawyers from identifying their clients without their consent, except in extraordinary circumstances. Rule 1.6 of the *Model Rules of Professional Conduct* provides that absent extraordinary circumstances, "[a] lawyer shall not reveal information relating to the representation of a client unless the client gives consent after consultation" – a prohibition that generally includes disclosure of a client's identity. *See* Ctr. For Prof'l Responsibility, Am. Bar Ass'n, Annotated Model Rules of Professional

Conduct 83 (4th ed. 1999). Because the decision ultimately belongs to the detainees and not their lawyers, providing a list of the lawyers' names would do little more to facilitate identification of the detainees than the government's current policy of allowing the detainees to identify themselves to the media and to whomever else they choose.

Even assuming that releasing attorneys' names will somehow facilitate identification of the detainees, the court's all-or-nothing approach again impermissibly shifts the burden of identifying exempt information from the government to plaintiffs. The government's Exemption 7(A) argument for withholding lawyers' names thus fails for the same reason as its 7(A) argument for withholding the names of all detainees. How would releasing the names of attorneys representing innocent clients with no connection to terrorist activities interfere with the government's terrorism investigation? Neither the court nor the government provides an explanation.

The government's second argument fares no better. The notion that the government must withhold the attorneys' names for their own good is flatly inconsistent with lawyers' roles as advocates and officers of the court in our fundamentally open legal system. Having voluntarily assumed this public role, lawyers have little expectation of anonymity. . . .

V.

Although I think it unreasonable to infer that all of the information plaintiffs seek in their FOIA request qualifies for exemption, the government may be able to point to more narrowly defined categories of information that might justify the inference. For example, while nothing in the record supports the government's contention that releasing the names of innocent detainees would harm the investigation, perhaps the government could justify withholding the places of arrest on the ground that such information might provide terrorist organizations with some insight into the government's investigative methods and strategy. I would therefore remand to allow the government to describe, for each detainee or reasonably defined category of detainees, on what basis it may withhold their names and other information. . . .

NOTES AND QUESTIONS

1. *Exemptions 7(C) and 7(F).* Because Judge Tatel dissented on Exemption 7(A), he also evaluated the government's alternative arguments that Exemptions 7(C) and 7(F) supported withholding the requested information:

Chapter 15. Public Access to National Security Information 115

Exemption 7(C) permits the government to withhold law enforcement records where their release "could reasonably be expected to constitute an unwarranted invasion of personal privacy." Like Exemption 7(A), the application of Exemption 7(C) is subject to a set of well established standards. Because the statute refers not to invasions of privacy generally, but to "unwarranted" invasions of privacy, courts evaluating claims for 7(C) exemption must do more than simply identify a privacy interest that will be compromised by disclosure of information. Instead, they must "balance the public interest in disclosure against the interest Congress intended the Exemption to protect." *Reporters Committee*, 489 U.S. at 776.

Relying on our decision in *Nation Magazine* [v. United States Customs Serv., 71 F.3d 885 (D.C. Cir. 1995)], the government argues that the detainees have "'an obvious privacy interest cognizable under Exemption 7(C) in keeping secret the fact that they were subjects of a law enforcement investigation,'" and that these privacy concerns are "particularly acute given the nature and magnitude of the September 11 attacks." This argument is unconvincing. For one thing, if the government is so concerned with the detainees' privacy, why has it released so much information about them? . . .

In any event, we have never held that individuals who have been not only investigated, but also arrested and jailed, have a similar privacy interest in avoiding "unwarranted association with criminal activity or reputational harm." *Nation Magazine*, 71 F.3d at 894. Even though being arrested subjects a person suspected of criminal activity to embarrassment and potentially more serious reputational harm, the law is nevertheless clear that no right of privacy "is violated by the disclosure of 'an official act such as an arrest.'" Am. Fed'n of Gov't Employees, AFL-CIO v. Dep't of Housing & Urban Dev., 118 F.3d 786, 794 (D.C. Cir. 1997).

To be sure, detainees may have a unique interest in avoiding association with the crimes of September 11. Even so, that interest is clearly outweighed by the public interest in knowing whether the government, in investigating those heinous crimes, is violating the rights of persons it has detained. And while FOIA asks only whether the public interest in disclosure outweighs the private interest in secrecy, it bears noting that the private interests in this case weigh on both sides of the balance: Plaintiffs' request for disclosure of the detainees' names seeks to vindicate not only the public's right to know what its government is up to, but also the detainees' own rights, including the right to counsel and to speedy trial. . . .

The government next invokes Exemption 7(F), which permits withholding law enforcement records where their release "could reasonably be expected to endanger the life or physical safety of any individual." Here again, the government's evidence fails to establish that the entire range of records encompassed in the plaintiffs' FOIA request "could reasonably be expected" to endanger the detainees.

The government's declarations tell us only that (1) "[d]etainees who are, in fact[,] affiliated with a terrorist group may be perceived by such groups as informants for the United States and be killed to preclude their future cooperation," Reynolds Decl. ¶37, and (2) "[i]f prisoners learn that an individual who was detained as a result of the investigation emanating from the September 11 attacks is in their own prison facility, some may try to retaliate against this individual," *id.* ¶29. The government tells us nothing about what threat, if any, disclosure would pose to detainees who are neither affiliated with a terrorist group nor currently imprisoned. And the government's own disclosures again undermine its assertions about detainees' safety. Plaintiffs point out that the Justice Department Inspector General himself named two of the detention centers used to house the terrorism investigation detainees, a fact that the government neither denies nor explains. Again, the government may have had reasons for disclosing the names of only these two detention centers, but nothing in the Reynolds declaration tells us what those reasons might be. . . . [331 F.3d at 945-948.]

Can you outline the government's response to Judge Tatel?

2. *Factual Predicates.* The court of appeals decision in the principal case rested in part on assumptions about the treatment of the detainees about whom information was sought. The Inspector General's Report on the detentions casts serious doubt on these assumptions. *See* p. 47 of this Supplement. Should the full court grant reconsideration in light of this report?

D. COMMON LAW RIGHT TO KNOW

Page 956. Add this material to the end of Note 1.

In the *CNSS* decision, *supra*, plaintiffs supplemented their FOIA claim for information about post-September 11 detainees by asserting a common law right to the same records. The government argued that the common law right is limited to judicial records and that, even if that right might otherwise apply to executive records, FOIA has displaced it. The court rejected the government's first argument but accepted the second one:

FOIA provides an extensive statutory regime for plaintiffs to request the information they seek. Not only is it uncontested that the requested information meets the general category of information for which FOIA mandates disclosure, but for the reasons set forth above, we have concluded that it falls within an express statutory exemption as well. It would make no sense for Congress to have enacted the balanced scheme

Chapter 15. Public Access to National Security Information   117

of disclosure and exemption, and for the court to carefully apply that statutory scheme, and then to turn and determine that the statute had no effect on a preexisting common law right of access. Congress has provided a carefully calibrated statutory scheme, balancing the benefits and harms of disclosure. That scheme preempts any preexisting common law right. . . . [331 F.3d at 936-937.]

Can you reconcile the *CNSS* court's conclusion with the statement in *Schwartz* that "we can find no inconsistency or conflict between the Freedom of Information Act and the common law rule"? Do you think Congress intended for FOIA to provide the exclusive means for access to executive branch records?

E. CONSTITUTIONAL RIGHT TO KNOW

Page 969. Add this material to Note 7.

The Pentagon dramatically revised its rules for press access to the battlefield during the 2003 war in Iraq. It "embedded" some 500 print and broadcast journalists into a number of military units and allowed them to accompany troops to the front. Embed "slots" were allocated to media organizations, 80 percent of them domestic, rather than to individual journalists. *See Public Affairs Guidance on Embedding Media,* Feb. 10, 2003 (*Guidelines*), http://www.defenselink.mil/news/Feb2003/d20030228pag.pdf. This arrangement was intended, according to a DOD spokesman, to accommodate the wishes of the media, and also to refute any misinformation about, say, civilian casualties that might be disseminated by Saddam Hussein. *See Deputy Assistant Secretary Whitman Interview with BBC TV,* DOD News, Apr. 18, 2003, *at* http://www.defenselink.mil/transcripts/2003/tr20030418-0142.html. Live television coverage from the battlefield was extensive, yet apparently none of the reporting "compromised significantly anything that was occurring or endangered personnel out there." *Id.*

In return for this extensive access, reporters were obliged to follow broad guidelines about what could be covered (e.g., "military targets and objectives previously under attack") and what could not (e.g., "information regarding future operations"). *Guidelines* ¶4. Unit commanders could "impose temporary restrictions on electronic transmissions for operational security reasons," and reporters had to "seek approval to use electronic devices in a combat/hostile environment." ¶2.C.4. Disputes about coverage of particular events were left to be worked out between reporters and unit commanders. ¶6. Commanders were to "ensure that media are provided with every opportunity to observe actual combat operations," but reporters could be given "escorts." ¶¶3.F., 3.G. There was no general review process for media products, as there was during the 1991 Persian Gulf War, but embargoes could be imposed "to protect operational security." ¶¶3.R., 4.E. The guidelines also included this enigmatic instruction: "Use of lipstick and helmet-mounted cameras on combat sorties is approved and encouraged to the greatest extent possible." ¶7.C.

No specific provision was made for "unilateral" journalists who were not embedded, except that they might be afforded a "different level of access." ¶3.T.

Page 970. Add these materials before Section F.

Detroit Free Press v. Ashcroft
United States Court of Appeals, Sixth Circuit, 2002
303 F.3d 681

KEITH, Circuit Judge. The primary issue on appeal in this case is whether the First Amendment to the United States Constitution confers a public right of access to deportation hearings. If it does, then the Government must make a showing to overcome that right.

No one will ever forget the egregious, deplorable, and despicable terrorist attacks of September 11, 2001. These were cowardly acts. In response, our government launched an extensive investigation into the attacks, future threats, conspiracies, and attempts to come. As part of this effort, immigration laws are prosecuted with increased vigor. The issue before us today involves these efforts.

The political branches of our government enjoy near-unrestrained ability to control our borders. "[T]hese are policy questions entrusted exclusively to the political branches of our government." Fiallo v. Bell, 430 U.S. 787, 798 (1977). Since the end of the 19th Century, our government has enacted immigration laws banishing, or deporting, non-citizens because of their race and their beliefs. While the Bill of Rights jealously protects citizens from such laws, it has never protected non-citizens facing deportation in the same way. In our democracy, based on checks and balances, neither the Bill of Rights nor the judiciary can second-guess government's choices. The only safeguard on this extraordinary governmental power is the public, deputizing the press as the guardians of their liberty. "An informed public is the most potent of all restraints upon misgovernment[.]" Grosjean v. Am. Press Co., 297 U.S. 233, 250 (1936). "[They] alone can here protect the values of democratic government." New

Chapter 15. Public Access to National Security Information 119

York Times v. United States, 403 U.S. 713, 728 (1971) (per curiam) (Stewart, J., concurring).

Today, the Executive Branch seeks to take this safeguard away from the public by placing its actions beyond public scrutiny. Against non-citizens, it seeks the power to secretly deport a class if it unilaterally calls them "special interest" cases. The Executive Branch seeks to uproot people's lives, outside the public eye, and behind a closed door. Democracies die behind closed doors. The First Amendment, through a free press, protects the people's right to know that their government acts fairly, lawfully, and accurately in deportation proceedings. When government begins closing doors, it selectively controls information rightfully belonging to the people. Selective information is misinformation. The Framers of the First Amendment "did not trust any government to separate the true from the false for us." Kleindienst v. Mandel, 408 U.S. 753, 773 (1972) (quoting Thomas v. Collins, 323 U.S. 516, 545 (Jackson, J., concurring)). They protected the people against secret government. . . .

I. Facts and Procedural History

On September 21, 2001, Chief Immigration Judge Michael Creppy issued a directive (the "Creppy directive") to all United States Immigration Judges requiring closure of special interest cases. The Creppy directive requires that all proceedings in such cases be closed to the press and public, including family members and friends. The Record of the Proceeding is not to be disclosed to anyone except a deportee's attorney or representative, "assuming the file does not contain classified information." "This restriction on information includes confirming or denying whether such a case is on the docket or scheduled for a hearing."

On December 19, 2002, Immigration Judge Elizabeth Hacker conducted a bond hearing for Rabih Haddad ("Haddad"), one such special interest case. Haddad was subject to deportation, having overstayed his tourist visa. The Government further suspects that the Islamic charity Haddad operates supplies funds to terrorist organizations. Haddad's family, members of the public, including Congressman John Conyers, and several newspapers sought to attend his deportation hearing. Without prior notice to the public, Haddad, or his attorney, courtroom security officers announced that the hearing was closed to the public and the press. Haddad was denied bail, detained, and has since been in the government's custody. Subsequent hearings, conducted on January 2 and 10, 2002, were also closed to the public and the press. Haddad has been transferred to Chicago for additional proceedings.

Haddad, several newspapers (the "Newspaper Plaintiffs"), and Congressman Conyers filed complaints for injunctive and declaratory relief, asserting claims under (1) the Administrative Procedures Act ("APA"), 5 U.S.C. §551 *et seq.;* (2) the Immigration and Nationality Act ("INA"), 8 U.S.C. §1101 *et seq.,* and the regulations promulgated thereunder, 8 C.F.R. §§3.27 & 240.10; and (3) the First and Fifth Amendments to the United States Constitution. . . .

III. Analysis

A. Likelihood of Success on the Merits

1. The Effect of the Government's Plenary Power Over Immigration

The Government argues that the district court erred in ruling that the government's plenary power over immigration did not warrant deferential review. We are unpersuaded by the Government's claim, which would require complete deference in all facets of immigration law, including non-substantive immigration laws that infringe upon the Constitution. We hold that the Constitution meaningfully limits non-substantive immigration laws and does not require special deference to the Government.

The Government's broad authority over immigration was first announced more than one-hundred years ago in The Chinese Exclusion Case, 130 U.S. 581 (1889). . . . This power was derived not from an express provision of the Constitution, but from powers incident to sovereignty. . . .

Even The Chinese Exclusion Case, however, acknowledged that Congress's power over immigration matters was limited by "the constitution itself." *Id.* at 604. Were we to adopt the Government's position, one would wonder whether and how the Constitution could limit the political branches' power over immigration matters. Similarly, that position would undercut the force of the First Amendment. "The dominant purpose of the First Amendment was to prohibit the widespread practice of governmental suppression of embarrassing information." *New York Times,* 403 U.S. at 723-24 (Douglas, J., concurring) (citations omitted). It would be ironic, indeed, to allow the Government's assertion of plenary power to transform the First Amendment from the great instrument of open democracy to a safe harbor from public scrutiny. In the words of Justice Murphy, "[such a] conclusion would make our constitutional safeguards transitory and discriminatory in nature. . . . [We] cannot agree that the framers of the Constitution meant to make such an empty mockery of human freedom." Bridges v. Wixon, 326 U.S. 135, 162 (1945) (Murphy,

J., concurring). As a result, the Government's stated position finds no authority in the Constitution and is untenable.

a. *The Government Interprets* Kleindienst *Too Broadly*

The Government's blanket reliance on *Kleindienst* ignores the varied aspects of immigration law. Immigration includes substantive laws over who may enter or remain in this country, laws governing procedural aspects of immigration hearings, and regulations on the mechanics of deportation. Although acknowledging the political branches' plenary power over all substantive immigration laws and non-substantive immigration laws that do not implicate constitutional rights, the Supreme Court has repeatedly allowed for meaningful judicial review of non-substantive immigration laws where constitutional rights are involved. *Kleindienst* did not change these long-standing traditions.

In *Kleindienst,* Ernest Mandel, a self-proclaimed "revolutionary Marxist" and Belgian citizen, sought entry into the United States to speak at a conference at Stanford University. *Kleindienst,* 408 U.S. at 756-59. Mandel applied for and was denied a non-immigrant visa under a blanket provision of the Immigration and Nationality Act, §212(a)(28), prohibiting the entrance of "anarchists" or "persons advocating the overthrow of the government." *Id.* at 759. In excluding Mandel, the Attorney General declined to exercise his discretionary authority to waive this prohibition. *Id.*

Several professors brought suit alleging a violation of their First Amendment rights. . . . The Court, while acknowledging that the professors' First Amendment rights were implicated, affirmed the decision denying Mandel a visa. The Court stated:

> [p]lenary congressional power to make policies and rules for exclusion of aliens has long been firmly established. In the case of an alien excludable under §212(a)(28), Congress has delegated conditional exercise of this power to the Executive. We hold that when the Executive exercises this power negatively on the basis of a facially legitimate and bona fide reason, the courts will neither look behind the exercise of that discretion, *nor test it by balancing its justification against the First Amendment interests* of those who seek personal communication with the applicant.

Id. at 769-70 (emphasis added).

Kleindienst differs from the present case in two important, and related, ways. First, *Kleindienst* involved a substantive immigration decision. The law and decision at issue determined who entered the United States. Here, the Creppy directive has no effect on the eventual outcome of the deportation hearings. Second, *Kleindienst,* although recognizing a constitutional right, did not give any weight to that right. It specifically declined to balance the First Amendment right against the government's plenary power, because the law was a substantive immigration law. Therefore, if the First Amendment limits non-substantive immigration laws, *Kleindienst* offers no authority that the Government's actions are entitled to deferential review – *Kleindienst* ignored the existence of the professors' First Amendment rights altogether. Nor does it offer authority that the First Amendment does not limit non-substantive immigration laws – *Kleindienst* involved a substantive immigration law. In a case such as this, where a non-substantive immigration law involving a constitutional right is at issue, the Supreme Court has always recognized the importance of that constitutional right, never deferring to an assertion of plenary authority.

b. *The Constitution, Including the First Amendment, Meaningfully Limits Non-Substantive Immigration Laws*

The Supreme Court has always interpreted the Constitution meaningfully to limit non-substantive immigration laws, without granting the Government special deference. First, the Supreme Court has explicitly stated that non-citizens are afforded "the same constitutional protections of due process that we accord citizens." Hellenic Lines Ltd. v. Rhoditis, 398 U.S. 306, 309 (1970) (citing Kwong Hai Chew v. Colding, 344 U.S. 590, 596 (1953) (stating that "once an alien lawfully enters and resides in this country he becomes invested with the rights guaranteed by the Constitution to all people within our borders.")).

As old as the first immigration laws of this country is the recognition that non-citizens, even if illegally present in the United States, are "persons" entitled to the Fifth Amendment right of due process in deportation proceedings. *See* Wong Wing [v. United States, 163 U.S. 228 (1896)], at 238 (recognizing Fifth Amendment right in deportation proceedings). . . .

More recently, the Supreme Court has again applied non-deferential review to non-substantive immigration law. In Zadvydas v. Davis, 533 U.S. 678 (2001), two non-citizens were being held indefinitely beyond the normal statutory-removal period of ninety days, because no country would accept them. A post-removal-period statute authorized such detention. The issue, however, was whether the post-removal statute authorized a detention indefinitely, or for a period reasonably necessary to secure removal. The language of the statute set no such limit. The Court read an implicit reasonableness limit into the statute to avoid "serious constitutional problems." *Id.* at 690. Significantly, the Court dismissed the government's argument that Congress's plenary power to create immigration law required

Chapter 15. Public Access to National Security Information 123

deference to the political branches' decision-making. *Id.* at 699-700. The Court repeated the mantra that the plenary power was "subject to important constitutional limitations." *Id.* at 695 (citing INS v. Chadha, 462 U.S. 919, 941-942 (1983); The Chinese Exclusion Case, 130 U.S. 581, 604 (1889)).

The Government correctly notes that the Court in *Zadvydas* twice indicated that it might be deferential in situations involving terrorism. *See id.* at 691, 696 ("noting that [t]he provision authorizing detention does not apply narrowly to 'a small segment of particularly dangerous individuals,' say suspected terrorists, but broadly to aliens ordered removed for many and various reasons, including tourist visa violations," and noting that "Neither do we consider terrorism or other special circumstances where special arguments might be made for forms of preventative detention and for heightened deference to the judgments of the political branches with respect to matters of national security."). However, nothing in *Zadvydas* indicates that given such a situation, the Court would defer to the political branches' determination of who belongs in that "small segment of particularly dangerous individuals" without judicial review of the individual circumstances of each case, something that the Creppy directive strikingly lacks. The Court repeated the importance of strong procedural protections when constitutional rights were involved . . . .

Importantly, the Creppy directive does not apply to "a small segment of particularly dangerous" information, but a broad, indiscriminate range of information, including information likely to be entirely innocuous. Similarly, no definable standards used to determine whether a case is of "special interest" have been articulated. Nothing in the Creppy directive counsels that it is limited to "a small segment of particularly dangerous individuals." In fact, the Government so much as argues that certain non-citizens known to have no links to terrorism will be designated "special interest" cases. Supposedly, closing a more targeted class would allow terrorists to draw inferences from which hearings are open and which are closed.

While we sympathize and share the Government's fear that dangerous information might be disclosed in some of these hearings, we feel that the ordinary process of determining whether closure is warranted on a case-by-case basis sufficiently addresses their concerns. Using this stricter standard does not mean that information helpful to terrorists will be disclosed, only that the Government must be more targeted and precise in its approach. Given the importance of the constitutional rights involved, such safeguards must be vigorously guarded, lest the First Amendment turn into another balancing test. In the words of Justice Black:

> The word "security" is a broad, vague generality whose contours should not be invoked to abrogate the fundamental law embodied in the First Amendment. The guarding of military and diplomatic secrets at the expense of informed representative government provides no real security for our Republic.

New York Times, 403 U.S. at 719 (Black, J., concurring). . . .

c. *The Government's Remaining Argument*

Finally, the Government argues that this distinction between substantive and non-substantive immigration laws "fails to acknowledge that procedural requirements often reflect, and encompass, substantive choices" and that it "makes no sense." This contention strikes us as profoundly undemocratic in that it ignores the basic concept of checks and balances. More fundamentally, though, were the political branches' decisions not subject to certain basic procedural requirements, the government could act arbitrarily and behind closed doors, leaving unsettled the lives of thousands of immigrants. Even though the political branches may have unfettered discretion to deport and exclude certain people, requiring the Government to account for their choices assures an informed public – a foundational principle of democracy. . . .

2. Applicability of *Richmond Newspapers*

We next consider whether the First Amendment affords the press and public a right of access to deportation hearings. The Newspaper Plaintiffs argue that the right of access should be governed by the standards set forth in Richmond Newspapers, Inc. v. Virginia, 448 U.S. 555 (1980), and its progeny. The Government, on the other hand, contends that *Richmond Newspapers* and its progeny are limited to judicial proceedings, and therefore, the standards articulated in these cases do not apply to deportation hearings, which are administrative proceedings. According to the Government, review of claims of access to administrative proceedings are governed by the more deferential standard articulated in Houchins v. KQED, Inc., 438 U.S. 1 (1978). The Government also argues that even if the standard articulated in *Richmond Newspapers* and its progeny is the appropriate test, the Newspaper Plaintiffs cannot demonstrate a right of access to deportation hearings by the standards articulated therein. . . .

Chapter 15. Public Access to National Security Information

a. Richmond Newspapers *Is a Test of General Applicability*

. . . [I]n repeatedly applying *Richmond Newspapers's* two-part "experience and logic" test to assess the merits of cases claiming First Amendment access rights to different government proceedings, it is clear that the Court has since moved away from its position in *Houchins* and recognizes that there is a limited constitutional right to some government information. . . .

The *Richmond Newspapers* two-part test has also been applied to particular proceedings outside the criminal judicial context, including administrative proceedings. . . . Thus, we reject the Government's assertion that a line has been drawn between judicial and administrative proceedings, with the First Amendment guaranteeing access to the former but not the latter. "[T]he First Amendment question cannot be resolved solely on the label we give the event, i.e., 'trial' or otherwise." [Press-Enterprise Co. v. Superior Court, 478 U.S. 1 (1986) (*Press-Enterprise II*)], at 7. Moreover, the Government cites no cases explicitly stating such a categorical distinction – that the political branches of government are completely immune from the First Amendment guarantee of access recognized in *Richmond Newspapers*. On the contrary, we believe that there is a limited First Amendment right of access to certain aspects of the executive and legislative branches. *See Richmond Newspapers*, 448 U.S. at 584 ("[T]he First Amendment protects the public and the press from abridgment of their rights of access to information about the operation of *their government, including the Judicial Branch.* . . .") (Stevens, J., concurring) (emphasis added). While the Government is free to argue that the particular historical and structural features of certain administrative proceedings do not satisfy the *Richmond Newspapers* two-part test, we find that there is no basis to argue that the test itself does not apply.

b. *If the Houchins Test Is Still Good Law, It Does Not Apply to Formal, Quasi-Judicial Proceedings, Like Deportation Proceedings*

Finally, to the extent that the standard in *Houchins* remains good law, we do not find *Houchins* applicable to the facts of the present case. Here, the Newspaper Plaintiffs seek access to a demonstrably quasi-judicial government administrative proceeding normally open to the public, as opposed to *Houchins,* where the plaintiffs sought access to a government facility normally restricted to the public. . . .

A deportation proceeding, although administrative, is an adversarial, adjudicative process, designed to expel non-citizens from this country. "[T]he ultimate individual stake in these proceedings is the same as or greater than in criminal or civil actions." *See N. Jersey Media Group, Inc. v. Ashcroft*, 205 F. Supp. 2d 288, 301 (D.N.J. 2002). . . .

. . . [T]he line of cases from *Richmond Newspapers* to *Press-Enterprise II* recognize that there is in fact a *limited* constitutional right to *some* government information and also provide a test of general applicability for making that determination. Accordingly, we must assess whether the Newspaper Plaintiffs enjoy a First Amendment right of access to deportation hearings under the two-part test of *Richmond Newspapers* and its progeny.

3. The Two-Part *Richmond Newspapers* Test

Under the two-part "experience and logic" test from *Richmond Newspapers,* we conclude that there is a First Amendment right of access to deportation proceedings. Deportation hearings, and similar proceedings, have traditionally been open to the public, and openness undoubtedly plays a significant positive role in this process.

a. *Deportation Proceedings Have Traditionally Been Accessible to the Public*

"[B]ecause a 'tradition of accessibility implies the favorable judgment of experience,' *Globe Newspaper* [Co. v. Superior Court, 457 U.S. 596 (1982)], at 605 (quoting *Richmond Newspapers,* 448 U.S. at 589 (Brennan, J., concurring)), we . . . consider . . . whether the place and process have historically been open to the press and general public." *Press-Enter. II,* 478 U.S. at 8.

The parties first dispute whether this inquiry requires a significantly long showing that the proceedings at issue were historically open, such as a common law tradition. The government cites *Richmond Newspapers* for the proposition that the tradition of open hearings must have existed from the time "when our organic laws were adopted," presumably at the adoption of the Bill of Rights. *See Richmond Newspapers,* 448 U.S. at 569. . . .

. . . [A]lthough historical context is important, a brief historical tradition might be sufficient to establish a First Amendment right of access where the beneficial effects of access to that process are overwhelming and uncontradicted. *See id.* Accordingly, the Supreme Court has called both prongs of the test "complimentary considerations." *Press-Enter. II,* 478 U.S. at 8. This comports with the Court's view that the First Amendment concerns "broad principles," *Globe Newspaper,* 457 U.S. at 604, applicable to contexts not known to the Framers. However, we are mindful that "[a] historical tradition of at least some duration is obviously necessary, . . . [or]

nothing would separate the judicial task of constitutional interpretation from the political task of enacting laws currently deemed essential." In re The Reporters Comm. for Freedom of the Press, 773 F.2d 1325, 1332 (D.C. Cir. 1985) (Scalia, J.).

Nonetheless, deportation proceedings historically have been open. Although exceptions may have been allowed, the general policy has been one of openness. The first general immigration act was enacted in 1882. *See Kleindienst,* 408 U.S. at 761. Repeatedly, Congress has enacted statutes closing exclusion hearings. None of these statutes, however, has ever required closure of deportation hearings. Since 1965, INS regulations have explicitly required deportation proceedings to be presumptively open. *See* 8 C.F.R. §3.27. Since that time, Congress has revised the Immigration and Nationality Act at least 53 times without indicating that the INS had judged their intent incorrectly.

Moreover, the history of immigration law informs Congress's legislation. Open hearings, apart from their value to the community, have long been considered to advance fairness to the parties. *See generally Richmond Newspapers,* 448 U.S. 555. Additionally, Congress has long been aware that deportees are constitutionally guaranteed greater procedural rights than those excluded upon initial entry. Therefore, Congress likely legislated key differences between both procedures accordingly.

Next, relying on Capital Cities Media, Inc. [v. Chester, 797 F.2d 1164 (3d Cir. 1986)], the Government impermissibly expands the relevant inquiry by arguing that there was no common law right of access to administrative proceedings. First, this argument ignores the fact that the modern administrative state is an entity unknown to the Framers of the First Amendment. This argument also fails to recognize the evolving nature of our government. Administrative proceedings come in all shapes and sizes. To the extent that we look to similar proceedings, we should look to proceedings that are similar in form and substance. . . .

As stated earlier, to paraphrase the Supreme Court, deportation hearings "walk, talk, and squawk" very much like a judicial proceeding. Substantively, we look to other proceedings that have the same effect as deportation. Here, the only other federal court that can enter an order of removal is a United States District Court during sentencing in a criminal trial. *See* 8 U.S.C.A. §1228(c) (2002). At common law, beginning with the Transportation Act of 1718, the English criminal courts could enter an order of transportation or banishment as a sentence in a criminal trial. As *Richmond Newspapers* discussed in great length, these types of criminal proceedings have historically been open. *Richmond Newspapers,* 448 U.S. at 564-74. . . .

b. *Public Access Plays a Significant Positive Role in Deportation Hearings*

Next, we turn to the "logic" prong, which asks "whether public access plays a significant positive role in the functioning of the particular process in question." *Press-Enter. II,* 478 U.S. at 8-9. Public access undoubtedly enhances the quality of deportation proceedings. Much of the reasoning from *Richmond Newspapers* is also applicable to this context.

First, public access acts as a check on the actions of the Executive by assuring us that proceedings are conducted fairly and properly. *See Richmond Newspapers,* 448 U.S. at 569 (noting that public access assures that proceedings are conducted fairly, including discouraging perjury, the misconduct of participants, and decisions based on secret bias or partiality). In an area such as immigration, where the government has nearly unlimited authority, the press and the public serve as perhaps the only check on abusive government practices.

Second, openness ensures that government does its job properly; that it does not make mistakes. "It is better that many [immigrants] should be improperly admitted than one natural born citizen of the United States should be permanently excluded from his country." *Kwock Jan Fat* [v. White, 253 U.S. 454 (1920)], at 464. . . .

Third, after the devastation of September 11 and the massive investigation that followed, the cathartic effect of open deportations cannot be overstated. They serve a "therapeutic" purpose as outlets for "community concern, hostility, and emotions." *Richmond Newspapers,* 448 U.S. at 571. . . .

Fourth, openness enhances the perception of integrity and fairness. "The value of openness lies in the fact that people not actually attending trials can have confidence that standards of fairness are being observed; the sure knowledge that *anyone* is free to attend gives assurance that established procedures are being followed and that deviations will become known." [Press-Enterprise Co. v. Superior Court, 464 U.S. 501 (1984)], at 508. The most stringent safeguards for a deportee "would be of limited worth if the public is not persuaded that the standards are being fairly enforced. Legitimacy rests in large part on public understanding." *See* First Amendment Coalition [v. Judicial Inquiry & Review Bd.], 784 F.2d [467 (3d Cir. 1986 (en banc)] at 486 (Adams, J., concurring in part, dissenting in part).

Fifth, public access helps ensure that "the individual citizen can effectively participate in and contribute to our republican system of self-government." *Globe Newspaper,* 457 U.S. at 604. "[A] major purpose of [the First Amendment] was to protect the free discussion of governmental

Chapter 15. Public Access to National Security Information

affairs." *Id.* Public access to deportation proceedings helps inform the public of the affairs of the government. Direct knowledge of how their government is operating enhances the public's ability to affirm or protest government's efforts. When government selectively chooses what information it allows the public to see, it can become a powerful tool for deception. . . .

Having found a First Amendment right of access to deportation hearings, we now determine whether the Government has made a sufficient showing to overcome that right.

4. Strict Scrutiny

Under the standard articulated in *Globe Newspaper*, government action that curtails a First Amendment right of access "in order to inhibit the disclosure of sensitive information" must be supported by a showing "that denial is necessitated by a compelling governmental interest, and is narrowly tailored to serve that interest." *Globe Newspaper Co.*, 457 U.S. at 606-07. Moreover, "[t]he interest is to be articulated along with findings specific enough that a reviewing court can determine whether the closure order was properly entered." *Press-Enter. II*, 478 U.S. at 10. The Government's ongoing anti-terrorism investigation certainly implicates a compelling interest. However, the Creppy directive is neither narrowly tailored, nor does it require particularized findings. Therefore, it impermissibly infringes on the Newspaper Plaintiffs' First Amendment right of access.

a. *The Government Cites Compelling Interests* . . .

Before the district court, the Government provided the affidavit of James S. Reynolds, Chief of the Terrorism and Violent Crimes Section of the Justice Department's Criminal Division, to explain the types of information that public access to removal proceedings would disclose. In his affidavit, Mr. Reynolds explained the rationale for prohibiting public access to the proceedings. . . .

The Government certainly has a compelling interest in preventing terrorism. In addition to Mr. Reynold's affidavit, other affidavits have been provided that justify the Government's interest in closure. According to the additional affidavits, public access to removal proceedings would disclose the following information that would impede the Government's investigation:

"Bits and pieces of information that may appear innocuous in isolation," but used by terrorist groups to help form a "bigger picture" of the Government's terrorism investigation, would be disclosed. The Government describes this type of intelligence gathering as "akin to the construction of a mosaic," where an individual piece of information is not of obvious importance until pieced together with other pieces of information. J. Roderick MacArthur Found. v. F.B.I., 102 F.3d 600, 604 (D.C. Cir. 1996).

See Gov't Brief at 47-49.

Inasmuch as these agents' declarations establish that certain information revealed during removal proceedings could impede the ongoing anti-terrorism investigation, we defer to their judgment. These agents are certainly in a better position to understand the contours of the investigation and the intelligence capabilities of terrorist organizations.

b. *The Creppy Directive Does Not Require Particularized Findings*

Although the Government is able to demonstrate a compelling interest for closure, the immigration judge, Defendant Hacker, failed to make specific findings before closing Haddad's deportation proceedings. *Press-Enterprise II* instructs that in cases where partial or complete closure is warranted, there must be specific findings on the record so that a reviewing court can determine whether closure was proper and whether less restrictive alternatives exist. *Press-Enter. II,* 478 U.S. at 13. Similarly, the Creppy directive fails this requirement.

c. *The Creppy Directive Is Not Narrowly Tailored*

Finally, the blanket closure rule mandated by the Creppy directive is not narrowly tailored. The Government offers no persuasive argument as to why the Government's concerns cannot be addressed on a case-by-case basis. The Newspaper Plaintiffs argue, and the district court agreed, that the Creppy directive is ineffective in achieving its purported goals because the detainees and their lawyers are allowed to publicize the proceedings. According to the Newspaper Plaintiffs, to the extent that Haddad had discussed his proceedings (and disclosed documents) with family, friends and the media, the information that the Government seeks to protect is disclosed to the public anyway. We are not persuaded by the Government's argument in response that few detainees will disclose any information and that their disclosure will be less than complete public access. This contention is, at best, speculative and belies the Government's assertion that *any* information disclosed, even bits and pieces that seem innocuous, will be detrimental to the anti-terrorism investigation.

The recent interim rule promulgated by the Department of Justice ("DOJ") regarding protective orders and sealing of documents in these special interest cases does not fully address our concern that the Creppy directive is under-inclusive. The parties do not dispute that the rule is meant to work in tandem with the Creppy directive. The interim DOJ rule authorizes immigration judges to issue protective orders and seal documents relating to law enforcement or national security information in the course of immigration proceedings. *See* 67 Fed. Reg. 36799. Pursuant to the interim rules, the immigration judge is authorized to order that detainees and their attorneys refrain from disclosing certain confidential information.

. . . [W]e construe the orders to terminate when the deportation proceedings end. At this juncture, nothing precludes the deportee from disclosing this information. Thus, the interim rule does not remedy the under-inclusiveness of the Creppy directive.

The interim rule notwithstanding, the Creppy directive is also over-inclusive, being too broad and indiscriminate. The Government contends that the closure mandated by the Creppy directive is narrowly tailored because "no less restrictive alternative would serve the Government's purpose." *See* United States v. Playboy, 529 U.S. 803, 815 (2000) ("[I]f a less restrictive means is available for the Government to achieve its goals, the Government must use it.").

It is clear that certain types of information that the Government seeks to keep confidential could be kept from the public on a case-by-case basis through protective orders or in camera review – for example, the identification of investigative sources and witnesses. The Government, however, argues that it is impossible to keep some sensitive information confidential if any portion of a hearing is open or if the immigration court conducts a hearing to determine if closure is proper. Stated differently, the Government argues that there is sensitive information that would be disclosed if closure occurred on a case-by-case basis. First, the Government contends that the identities of the detainees would be revealed if closure occurred on a case-by-case basis, and such information would impede the anti-terrorism investigation. This information, however, is already being disclosed to the public through the detainees themselves or their counsel. Even if, as a result of the interim rule, a detainee remains silent, a terrorist group capable of sophisticated intelligence-gathering would certainly be made aware that one of its operatives, or someone connected to a particular terrorist plot, has disappeared into the Government's custody. Moreover, if a deportee does have links to terrorist organizations, there is nothing to stop that deportee from divulging the information learned from these proceedings once deported.

Next, the Government argues that open hearings would reveal the amount of intelligence that the Government does not possess. The Government argues that evidence concerning a particular detainee could be incomplete, and an incomplete presentation of evidence would permit terrorist groups to gauge how much the Government knows and does not know about their operations. The issue in a removal hearing is, however, narrowly focused, and the Government has enormous control over what evidence it introduces. "To deport an overstay, the INS must convince the immigration judge by clear and convincing evidence that the alien was admitted as a non-immigrant for a specific period, that the period has elapsed, and that the alien is still in this country." Shahla v. INS, 749 F.2d 561, 563 (9th Cir. 1984).

Here, the Government has detained Haddad and instituted removal proceedings based on his overstay of a tourist visa. Thus, the Government need only establish that Haddad obtained a visa, the visa has expired, and that he is still in the country. Very little information is required. The fact that the Government may have to contest the non-citizen's application for discretionary relief is similarly unavailing. At oral argument, it was brought to our attention that Haddad intends to apply for asylum, a form of discretionary relief available to non-citizens in deportation proceedings. We see no reason why, in making its case against the applicant's request for discretionary relief, the Government could not seek to keep confidential, pertinent information, as the need arises.

Finally, the Government seeks to protect from disclosure the bits and pieces of information that seem innocuous in isolation, but when pieced together with other bits and pieces aid in creating a bigger picture of the Government's anti-terrorism investigation, i.e., the "mosaic intelligence." Mindful of the Government's concerns, we must nevertheless conclude that the Creppy directive is over-inclusive. While the risk of "mosaic intelligence" may exist, we do not believe speculation should form the basis for such a drastic restriction of the public's First Amendment rights. *See Press-Enter. II,* 478 U.S. at 13 ("Since a qualified First Amendment right of access attaches . . ., the proceeding cannot be closed unless *specific, on the record findings are made* demonstrating that closure is *essential to preserve higher values* and is narrowly tailored to serve that interest."). Fittingly, in this case, the Government subsequently admitted that there was no information disclosed in any of Haddad's first three hearings that threatened "national security or the safety of the American people." U.S. Dept. of Justice, *Statement of Associate Attorney General Jay Stephens Regarding the Sixth Circuit Decision in the Haddad Case,* (last modified

Chapter 15. Public Access to National Security Information

8/20/02) <http://www.usdoj.gov/opa/pr/2002/April/02_ag_238.htm>. Yet, all these hearings were closed. The only reason offered for closing the hearings has been that the presiding immigration judge was told [to] do it by the chief immigration judge, who in turn was told to do it by the Attorney General.

Furthermore, there seems to be no limit to the Government's argument. The Government could use its "mosaic intelligence" argument as a justification to close any public hearing completely and categorically, including criminal proceedings. The Government could operate in virtual secrecy in all matters dealing, even remotely, with "national security," resulting in a wholesale suspension of First Amendment rights. By the simple assertion of "national security," the Government seeks a process where it may, without review, designate certain classes of cases as "special interest cases" and, behind closed doors, adjudicate the merits of these cases to deprive non-citizens of their fundamental liberty interests.

This, we simply may not countenance. A government operating in the shadow of secrecy stands in complete opposition to the society envisioned by the Framers of our Constitution. "[F]ully aware of both the need to defend a new nation and the abuses of the English and Colonial governments, [the Framers of the First Amendment] sought to give this new society strength and security by providing that freedom of speech, press, religion, and assembly should not be abridged." *See New York Times,* 403 U.S. at 719 (Black, J., concurring).

Moreover, we find unpersuasive the Government's argument that the closure of special interest hearings has been accomplished on a case-by-case basis. In its reply, the Government alleges that "[e]ach special interest detainee has been evaluated and designated on the basis of the government's ongoing investigative interest in him and his relationship to the ongoing anti-terrorism investigation." Assuming such an evaluation has occurred, we find that problems still remain. The task of designating a case special interest is performed in secret, without any established standards or procedures, and the process is, thus, not subject to any sort of review, either by another administrative entity or the courts. Therefore, no real safeguard on this exercise of authority exists. "Civil liberties, as guaranteed by the Constitution, imply the existence of an organized society maintaining public order without which liberty itself would be lost in the excesses of unrestrained abuses." United States v. United States District Court, 407 U.S. 297, 312 (1972) (quoting Cox v. New Hampshire, 312 U.S. 569, 574 (1941)). The Government states that special interest cases represent "a small, carefully chosen subset of the universe of aliens facing removal proceedings." Yet, to date, the Government has failed to disclose the actual number of special interest cases it has designated.

In sum, we find that the Government's attempt to establish a narrowly tailored restriction has failed. The Creppy directive is under-inclusive by permitting the disclosure of sensitive information while at the same time drastically restricting First Amendment rights. The directive is over-inclusive by categorically and completely closing all special interest hearings without demonstrating, beyond speculation, that such a closure is absolutely necessary. . . .

Lastly, the public's interests are best served by open proceedings. A true democracy is one that operates on faith – faith that government officials are forthcoming and honest, and faith that informed citizens will arrive at logical conclusions. This is a vital reciprocity that America should not discard in these troubling times. Without question, the events of September 11, 2001, left an indelible mark on our nation, but we as a people are united in the wake of the destruction to demonstrate to the world that we are a country deeply committed to preserving the rights and freedoms guaranteed by our democracy. Today, we reflect our commitment to those democratic values by ensuring that our government is held accountable to the people and that First Amendment rights are not impermissibly compromised. Open proceedings, with a vigorous and scrutinizing press, serve to ensure the durability of our democracy.

IV. Conclusion

For the foregoing reasons, we AFFIRM.

North Jersey Media Group, Inc. v. Ashcroft
United States Court of Appeals, Third Circuit, 2002
308 F.3d 198, *cert. denied,* 123 S. Ct. 2215 (2003)

BECKER, Chief Judge. This civil action was brought in the District Court for the District of New Jersey by a consortium of media groups seeking access to "special interest" deportation hearings involving persons whom the Attorney General has determined might have connections to or knowledge of the September 11, 2001 terrorist attacks. This category was created by a directive issued by Michael Creppy, the Chief United States Immigration Judge, outlining additional security measures to be applied in this class of cases, including closing hearings to the public and the press. Named as defendants in the suit were Attorney General John Ashcroft and Chief Judge Creppy. The District Court found for the media plaintiffs and

Chapter 15. Public Access to National Security Information 135

issued an order enjoining the Attorney General from denying access, from which he now appeals. . . .

As we will now explain in detail, we find that the application of the *Richmond Newspapers* [Richmond Newspapers, Inc. v. Virginia, 448 U.S. 555 (1980)] experience and logic tests does not compel us to declare the Creppy Directive unconstitutional. We will therefore reverse the Order of the District Court.

I. BACKGROUND

A. The Creppy Directive . . .

In closing special interest deportation hearings, the Government's stated purpose is to avoid disclosing potentially sensitive information to those who may pose an ongoing security threat to the United States and its interests. The Government represents that "if evidence is offered about a particular phone number link between a detainee and a number connected to a terrorist organization or member," the terrorists "will be on notice that the United States is now aware of the link" and "may even be able to determine what sources and methods the United States used to become aware of that link." (Watson Declaration) Equally important, however, is "information that might appear innocuous in isolation [but that] can be fit into a bigger picture by terrorist groups in order to thwart the Government's efforts to investigate and prevent terrorism." (*Id.*) For example, information about how and why special interest aliens were detained "would allow the terrorist organizations to discern patterns and methods of investigation"; information about how such aliens entered the country "would allow the terrorist organization to see patterns of entry, what works and what doesn't"; and information "about what evidence the United States has against members of a particular cell collectively" would reveal to the terrorist organization which of its cells have been significantly compromised. (*Id.*)

The Government offers a litany of harms that might flow from open hearings. Most obviously, terrorist organizations could alter future attack plans, or devise new, easier ways to enter the country through channels they learn are relatively unguarded by the Department of Justice. They might also obstruct or disrupt pending proceedings by destroying evidence, threatening potential witnesses, or targeting the hearings themselves. Finally, if the government cannot guarantee a closed hearing, aliens might be deterred from cooperating with the ongoing investigation. *See infra.* . . .

II. APPLICABILITY OF *RICHMOND NEWSPAPERS* . . .

While we agree with the District Court's conclusion that *Richmond Newspapers* analysis is proper in the administrative context, we disagree with its application and hold that under that test, there is no First Amendment right to attend deportation proceedings.

A. *Applicability to Article III Proceedings*

. . . The *Richmond Newspapers* First Amendment right of access to criminal trials . . . stemmed from an "uncontradicted history, supported by reasons as valid today as in centuries past." *Id.* at 573. In his pragmatic concurrence, Justice Brennan concluded that:

> [T]wo helpful principles may be sketched. First, the case for a right of access has special force when drawn from an enduring and vital tradition of public entree to particular proceedings or information. Such a tradition commands respect in part because the Constitution carries the gloss of history. More importantly, a tradition of accessibility implies the favorable judgment of experience. Second, the value of access must be measured in specifics. Analysis is not advanced by rhetorical statements that all information bears upon public issues; what is crucial in individual cases is whether access to a particular government process is important in terms of that very process.

Id. at 589.

Despite Justice O'Connor's admonition that *Richmond Newspapers* does not have "any implications outside the context of criminal trials," *Globe Newspaper Co. v. Superior Court,* 457 U.S. 596, 611 (1982), a majority of the Court has since adopted Justice Brennan's language as a test of at least somewhat broader application. In *Press-Enterprise Co. v. Superior Court,* 478 U.S. [1 (1986)] (*Press-Enterprise II*), the Court held that there is a First Amendment right of access to preliminary hearings. *Id.* at 13. In so doing, it formalized what has come to be known as the *Richmond Newspapers* "experience and logic" test:

> First, because a tradition of accessibility implies the favorable judgment of experience, we have considered whether the place and process have historically been open to the press and general public. . . . Second, in this setting the Court has traditionally considered whether public access plays a significant positive role in the functioning of the particular process in question.

Id. at 8 (citations omitted). The Court recognized that "[t]hese considerations of experience and logic are, of course, related, for history and experience shape the functioning of governmental processes." *Id.* at 9. Nevertheless, it made clear that relation is not tantamount to equivalence, and it independently applied both prongs of the test to preliminary proceedings. . . .

B. Applicability of Richmond Newspapers to Administrative Proceedings

The Government contends that while *Richmond Newspapers* properly applies to civil and criminal proceedings under Article III, the Constitution's text militates against extending First Amendment rights to non-Article III proceedings such as deportation. Its premise is one of *expressio unius est exclusio alterius:* Article III is silent on the question of public access to judicial trials, but the Sixth Amendment expressly incorporates the common law tradition of public trials, thus supporting the notion that the First Amendment likewise incorporates that tradition for Article III purposes. Articles I and II, conversely, *do* address the question of access, and they *do not* provide for Executive or Legislative proceedings to be open to the public. To the Government, the absence of an explicit guarantee of access for Article I and II proceedings (as exists in Article III) gives rise to a distinction with a difference because, without an incorporating provision parallel to the Sixth Amendment, the Framers must have intended to deny the public access to political proceedings.

The Government's suggestion is ultimately that we should not apply *Richmond Newspapers* where the Constitution's structure dictates that no First Amendment right applies, and should instead let the political branches (here, the Executive, acting through the Justice Department) determine the proper degree of access to administrative proceedings.

Our own jurisprudence precludes this approach. In *Publicker* [Industries, Inc. v. Cohen, 733 F.2d 1059 (3d Cir. 1984)], for example, we found a First Amendment right to attend civil trials, proceedings to which the Sixth Amendment is entirely inapplicable. . . .

. . . [I]n this Court, *Richmond Newspapers* is a test broadly applicable to issues of access to government proceedings, including removal. In this one respect we note our agreement with the Sixth Circuit's conclusion in their nearly identical case. *See Detroit Free Press v. Ashcroft,* 303 F.3d 681 (6th Cir. 2002). We now employ that test to determine whether the press and public have a First Amendment right to attend deportation hearings.

III. UNDER *RICHMOND NEWSPAPERS,* IS THERE A FIRST AMENDMENT RIGHT TO ATTEND DEPORTATION HEARINGS? . . .

A. The "Experience" Test

1. Is there an historical right of access to government proceedings generally?

In *Richmond Newspapers,* 448 U.S. at 575, the Supreme Court acknowledged the State's argument that the Constitution nowhere explicitly guarantees the public's right to attend criminal trials, but it found that right implicit because the Framers drafted the Constitution against a backdrop of longstanding popular access to criminal trials. Likewise, in *Publicker,* 733 F.2d at 1059, we found a First Amendment right of access to civil trials because at common law, such access had been "beyond dispute."

The history of access to political branch proceedings is quite different. The Government correctly notes that the Framers themselves rejected any unqualified right of access to the political branches for, as we explained in *Capital Cities Media* [Inc. v. Chester, 797 F.2d 1164 (3d Cir. 1986], at 1168-1171, the evidence on this point is extensive and compelling. . . .

This tradition of closing sensitive proceedings extends to many hearings before administrative agencies. For example, although hearings on Social Security disability claims profoundly affect hundreds of thousands of people annually, and have great impact on expenditure of government funds, they are open only to "the parties and to other persons the administrative law judge considers necessary and proper." 20 C.F.R. §404.944. Likewise, administrative disbarment hearings are often presumptively closed. . . .

Faced with this litany of administrative hearings that are closed to the public, the Newspapers cannot claim a general First Amendment right of access to government proceedings without urging a judicially-imposed revolution in the administrative state. They wisely avoid that tactic, at least directly. Instead they submit that, despite frequent closures throughout the administrative realm, deportation proceedings in particular boast a history of openness sufficient to meet the *Richmond Newspapers* requirement. We now assess that claim, and find that we disagree.

Chapter 15. Public Access to National Security Information 139

2. **Is the history of open deportation proceedings sufficient to satisfy the *Richmond Newspapers* "experience" prong?**

For a First Amendment right of access to vest under *Richmond Newspapers*, we must consider whether "the place and process have historically been open to the press and general public," because such a "tradition of accessibility implies the favorable judgment of experience." *Press-Enterprise II,* 478 U.S. at 8. Noting preliminarily that the question whether a proceeding has been "historically open" is only arguably an objective inquiry, we nonetheless find that based on both Supreme Court and Third Circuit precedents, the tradition of open deportation hearings is too recent and inconsistent to support a First Amendment right of access.

The strongest historical evidence of open deportation proceedings is that since the 1890s, when Congress first codified deportation procedures, "[t]he governing statutes have always expressly closed *exclusion* hearings, but have *never* closed deportation hearings." (Newspapers' Br. at 30- 31.) In 1893, the Executive promulgated the first set of immigration regulations, which expressly stated that exclusion proceedings shall be conducted "separate from the public." *See* Treasury Dept., *Immigration Laws and Regulations* 4 (Washington D.C., Gov't Printing Office 1893). Congress codified those regulations in 1903 and, since that time, it has repeatedly reenacted provisions closing exclusion hearings. In contrast, although Congress codified the regulations governing deportation proceedings in 1904 and has reenacted them many times since, it has never authorized the general closure that has long existed in the exclusion context.

The Newspapers submit that under the rule of construction *expressio unius est exclusio alterius,* Congress's practice of closing exclusion proceedings while remaining silent on deportation proceedings creates a presumption that it intended deportation proceedings to be open. In support of this interpretation, they point out that the current Justice Department regulations provide explicitly that "[a]ll hearings, other than exclusion hearings, shall be open to the public except that . . . [f]or the purpose of protecting . . . the public interest, the Immigration Judge may limit attendance or hold a closed hearing." 8 C.F.R. §3.27. From this they conclude that the regulations state explicitly what the statutes had long said implicitly, namely that deportation hearings are to be open unless an individualized case is made for closure.

But there is also evidence that, in practice, deportation hearings have frequently been closed to the general public. From the early 1900s, the government has often conducted deportation hearings in prisons, hospitals, or private homes, places where there is no general right of public access. Even in recent times, the government has continued to hold thousands of deportation hearings each year in federal and state prisons. Moreover, hearings involving abused alien children are closed by regulation no matter where they are held, and those involving abused alien spouses are closed presumptively. *See* 8 C.F.R. §3.27(c).

We ultimately do not believe that deportation hearings boast a tradition of openness sufficient to satisfy *Richmond Newspapers*. In *Richmond Newspapers* itself, the Court noted an "unbroken, uncontradicted history" of public access to criminal trials in Anglo American law running from "before the Norman Conquest" to the present, and it emphasized that it had not found "a single instance of a criminal trial conducted in camera in any federal, state, or municipal court during the history of this country." 448 U.S. at 565, 572, 573 & n. 9. Likewise, in *Publicker,* 733 F.2d at 1059, we found that access to civil trials at common law was "beyond dispute."

The tradition of open deportation hearings is simply not comparable. While the *expressio unius* distinction between exclusion and deportation proceedings is a tempting road to travel, we are unwilling effectively to craft a constitutional right from mere Congressional silence, especially when faced with evidence that some deportation proceedings were, and are, explicitly closed to the public or conducted in places unlikely to allow general public access. Although the 1964 Department of Justice regulations did create a presumption of openness, a recent – and rebuttable – regulatory presumption is hardly the stuff of which Constitutional rights are forged. . . .

3. Relaxing the *Richmond Newspapers* experience requirement would lead to perverse consequences.

. . . [T]here is no fundamental right of access to administrative proceedings. Any such access, therefore, must initially be granted as a matter of executive grace. The Government contends that by relaxing the need for a "1000-year tradition of public access," (Gov't Br. at 35), we would permanently constitutionalize a right of access whenever an executive agency does not consistently bar all public access to a particular proceeding. We do not adopt this reasoning in its entirety, for as we have discussed *supra,* we have sometimes found a constitutional right of access to proceedings that did not exist at common law.

Nevertheless, we agree with the Government that a rigorous experience test is necessary to preserve the "basic tenet of administrative law that agencies should be free to fashion their own rules of procedure." *Vermont Yankee Nuclear Power Corp. v. Natural Resources Defense Council, Inc.,* 435 U.S. 519, 544 (1978). Were we to adopt the Newspapers' view that we can recognize a First Amendment right based solely on the logic prong if

Chapter 15. Public Access to National Security Information   141

there is no history of closure, we would effectively compel the Executive to close its proceedings to the public *ab initio* or risk creating a constitutional right of access that would preclude it from closing them in the future. Under such a system, reserved powers of closure would be meaningless. It seems possible that, ironically, such a system would result in less public access than one in which a constitutional right of access is more difficult to create.

At all events, we would find this outcome incredible in an area of traditional procedural flexibility, and we are unwilling to reach it when a reasonable alternative is present. By insisting on a strong tradition of public access in the *Richmond Newspapers* test, we preserve administrative flexibility and avoid constitutionalizing ambiguous, and potentially unconsidered, executive decisions.

IV. DOES THE *RICHMOND NEWSPAPERS* "LOGIC" PRONG, PROPERLY APPLIED, SUPPORT A RIGHT OF ACCESS?

Even if we could find a right of access under the *Richmond Newspapers* logic prong, absent a strong showing of openness under the experience prong, a proposition we do not embrace, we would find no such right here. The logic test compels us to consider "whether public access plays a significant positive role in the functioning of the particular process in question." *Press-Enterprise II,* 478 U.S. at 8. . . .

In *Press-Enterprise II,* the case that formalized the *Richmond Newspapers* test, the Court identified several reasons that openness plays a significant positive role in preliminary hearings. It recognized that "[b]ecause of its extensive scope, the preliminary hearing is often the final and most important step in the criminal proceeding," and in many cases it "provides the sole occasion for public observation of the criminal justice system." *Id.* at 12 (citation omitted). Similarly, it found that "the absence of a jury, long recognized as an inestimable safeguard against the corrupt or overzealous prosecutor and against the compliant, biased, or eccentric judge, makes the importance of public access to a preliminary hearing even more significant." *Id.* at 12-13 (citations omitted). Summarizing that "[d]enying the transcript of a [ ] preliminary hearing would frustrate what we have characterized as the 'community therapeutic value' of openness," it concluded that a qualified First Amendment right of access attaches to preliminary hearings. *Id.* at 13. . . .

We agree with the District Court and the Sixth Circuit that openness in deportation hearings performs each of these salutary functions, but we are troubled by our sense that the logic inquiry, as currently conducted, does not do much work in the *Richmond Newspapers* test. We have not found a case in which a proceeding passed the experience test through its history of openness yet failed the logic test by not serving community values. Under the reported cases, whenever a court has found that openness serves community values, it has concluded that openness plays a "significant positive role" in that proceeding. But that cannot be the story's end, for to gauge accurately whether a role is positive, the calculus must perforce take account of the flip side – the extent to which openness impairs the public good. We note in this respect that, were the logic prong only to determine whether openness serves some good, it is difficult to conceive of a government proceeding to which the public would not have a First Amendment right of access. For example, public access to *any* government affair, even internal CIA deliberations, would "promote informed discussion" among the citizenry. It is unlikely the Supreme Court intended this result.

In this case the Government presented substantial evidence that open deportation hearings would threaten national security. Although the District Court discussed these concerns as part of its strict scrutiny analysis, they are equally applicable to the question whether openness, on balance, serves a positive role in removal hearings. We find that upon factoring them into the logic equation, it is doubtful that openness promotes the public good in this context.

The Government's security evidence is contained in the declaration of Dale Watson, the FBI's Executive Assistant Director for Counterterrorism and Counterintelligence. Watson presents a range of potential dangers, the most pressing of which we [d]escribe here.

First, public hearings would necessarily reveal sources and methods of investigation. That is information which, "when assimilated with other information the United States may or may not have in hand, allows a terrorist organization to build a picture of the investigation." (Watson Dec. at 4.) Even minor pieces of evidence that might appear innocuous to us would provide valuable clues to a person within the terrorist network, clues that may allow them to thwart the government's efforts to investigate and prevent future acts of violence. *Id.*

Second, "information about how any given individual entered the country (from where, when, and how) may not divulge significant information that would reveal sources and methods of investigation. However, putting entry information into the public realm regarding all 'special interest cases' would allow the terrorist organization to see patterns of entry, what works and what doesn't." *Id.* That information would allow it to tailor future entries to exploit weaknesses in the United States immigration system.

Third, "[i]nformation about what evidence the United States has against members of a particular cell collectively will inform the terrorist organization as to what cells to use and which not to use for further plots and attacks." *Id.* A related concern is that open hearings would reveal what evidence the government lacks. For example, the United States may disclose in a public hearing certain evidence it possesses about a member of a terrorist organization. If that detainee is actually involved in planning an attack, opening the hearing might allow the organization to know that the United States is not yet aware of the attack based on the evidence it presents at the open hearing. *Id.*

Fourth, if a terrorist organization discovers that a particular member is detained, or that information about a plot is known, it may accelerate the timing of a planned attack, thus reducing the amount of time the government has to detect and prevent it. If acceleration is impossible, it may still be able to shift the planned activity to a yet-undiscovered cell. *Id.* at 7.

Fifth, a public hearing involving evidence about terrorist links could allow terrorist organizations to interfere with the pending proceedings by creating false or misleading evidence. Even more likely, a terrorist might destroy existing evidence or make it more difficult to obtain, such as by threatening or tampering with potential witnesses. Should potential informants not feel secure in coming forward, that would greatly impair the ongoing investigation. *Id.* . . .

Finally, Watson represents that "the government cannot proceed to close hearings on a case-by-case basis, as the identification of certain cases for closure, and the introduction of evidence to support that closure, could itself expose critical information about which activities and patterns of behavior merit such closure." (Watson Dec. at 8-9.) Moreover, he explains, given judges' relative lack of expertise regarding national security and their inability to see the mosaic, we should not entrust to them the decision whether an isolated fact is sensitive enough to warrant closure.

The Newspapers are undoubtedly correct that the representations of the Watson Declaration are to some degree speculative, at least insofar as there is no concrete evidence that closed deportation hearings have prevented, or will prevent, terrorist attacks.[14] But the *Richmond Newspapers* logic prong

---

14. The Newspapers contend that speculative evidence is insufficient to withstand strict scrutiny. *See Press-Enterprise II,* 478 U.S. at 13 (requiring "specific, on the record findings"); *Globe Newspaper,* 457 U.S. 596, 609 (1982) (finding government interest insufficient to merit closure without accompanying empirical support). While we acknowledge the force of this contention, strict

is unavoidably speculative, for it is impossible to weigh objectively, for example, the community benefit of emotional catharsis against the security risk of disclosing the United States' methods of investigation and the extent of its knowledge. We are quite hesitant to conduct a judicial inquiry into the credibility of these security concerns, as national security is an area where courts have traditionally extended great deference to Executive expertise. *See, e.g., Zadvydas v. Davis,* 533 U.S. 678, 696 (2001) (noting that "terrorism or other special circumstances" might warrant "heightened deference to the judgments of the political branches with respect to matters of national security"). *See also Dep't of the Navy v. Egan,* 484 U.S. 518, 530 (1988) (noting that "courts traditionally have been reluctant to intrude upon the authority of the Executive in military and national security affairs"). The assessments before us have been made by senior government officials responsible for investigating the events of September 11th and for preventing future attacks. These officials believe that closure of special interest hearings is necessary to advance these goals, and their concerns, as expressed in the Watson Declaration, have gone unrebutted. To the extent that the Attorney General's national security concerns seem credible, we will not lightly second-guess them.

We are keenly aware of the dangers presented by deference to the executive branch when constitutional liberties are at stake, especially in times of national crisis, when those liberties are likely in greatest jeopardy. On balance, however, we are unable to conclude that openness plays a positive role in special interest deportation hearings at a time when our nation is faced with threats of such profound and unknown dimension.

V. CONCLUSION

Whatever the outer bounds of *Richmond Newspapers* might be, they do not envelop us here. Deportation proceedings' history of openness is quite limited, and their presumption of openness quite weak. They plainly do not present the type of "unbroken, uncontradicted history" that *Richmond Newspapers* and its progeny require to establish a First Amendment right of access. We do not decide that there is no right to attend administrative proceedings, or even that there is no right to attend any immigration proceeding. Our judgment is confined to the extremely narrow class of deportation cases that are determined by the Attorney General to present

---

scrutiny is appropriate only after finding a First Amendment right. Because we find no such right to attend deportation hearings, the speculative nature is not fatal.

Chapter 15. Public Access to National Security Information 145

significant national security concerns. In recognition [of] his experience (and our lack of experience) in this field, we will defer to his judgment. We note that although there may be no judicial remedy for these closures, there is, as always, the powerful check of political accountability on Executive discretion. . . .

Because we find that open deportation hearings do not pass the two-part *Richmond Newspapers* test, we hold that the press and public possess no First Amendment right of access. In the absence of such a right, we need not reach the subsequent questions whether the Creppy Directive's closures would pass a strict scrutiny analysis and whether the District Court's "national in scope" injunction was too broad.

The judgment of the District Court will be reversed.

[The opinion of SCIRICA, Circuit Judge, dissenting, is omitted.]

NOTES AND QUESTIONS

1. *Closing the Door on Democracy?* How would you compare the general attitudes of the Third and Sixth Circuit courts about their roles in cases implicating the national security? What specifically do you see in the two opinions that reveals a difference in attitudes?

Which court do you think struck the better balance between the public's interest in openness and the risk to national security, and why?

How much importance do you think the *North Jersey Media* court attached to government assertions that some "special interest" cases involved aliens associated with Al Qaeda or with the September 11 hijackers? Should the court have demanded proof of these assertions? Do you suppose that any such persons were actually deported?

Because of the importance of these cases, as well as the sharp split between the circuits, many were surprised by the Supreme Court's decision to deny certiorari in the *North Jersey Media* case. What, if anything, do you think this portends for First Amendment-based access to government activities and information in the future?

2. *The Detainees Redux.* In the *CNSS* decision (p. 101 in this Supplement), the court considered and rejected First Amendment grounds for releasing the names of the detainees. *Richmond Newspapers* was central to the First Amendment portion of the decision, and the court sought to distinguish the *Detroit Free Press* case:

Plaintiffs characterize the information they seek as "arrest records," and contend that the public has a right of access to arrest records under the First Amendment, as interpreted in *Richmond Newspapers*. We disagree. Plaintiffs seek not individual arrest records, but a comprehensive listing of the individuals detained in connection with a specified law enforcement investigation as well as investigatory information about where and when each individual was arrested, held, and released. The narrow First Amendment right of access to information recognized in *Richmond Newspapers* does not extend to non-judicial documents that are not part of a criminal trial, such as the investigatory documents at issue here. . . .

Neither the Supreme Court nor this Court has applied the *Richmond Newspapers* test outside the context of criminal judicial proceedings or the transcripts of such proceedings. When the "experience and logic" test has been applied beyond the trial itself, as in *Press-Enterprise II*, it has been limited to judicial proceedings that are part of the criminal trial process. . . .

We will not convert the First Amendment right of access to criminal judicial proceedings into a requirement that the government disclose information compiled during the exercise of a quintessential executive power – the investigation and prevention of terrorism. The dangers which we have catalogued above of making such release in this case provide ample evidence of the need to follow this course. To be sure, the Sixth Circuit recently held that the public has a constitutional right of access to INS deportation hearings involving the same INS detainees at issue in this case. *See Detroit Free Press; but see North Jersey Media Group* (finding no right of access). However, the Sixth Circuit applied *Richmond Newspapers* only after extensively examining the similarity between deportation proceedings and criminal trials, *Detroit Free Press*, 303 F.3d at 696-99, and noting the crucial distinction between "*investigatory* information" and "access to information relating to a governmental *adjudicative* process," *id.* at 699. Inasmuch as plaintiffs here request investigatory – not adjudicative – information, we find *Detroit Free Press* distinguishable. We therefore will not expand the First Amendment right of public access to require disclosure of information compiled during the government's investigation of terrorist acts. [*CNSS*, 331 F.3d at 933-934.]

Are you persuaded by the *CNSS* court's application of *Richmond Newspapers*? By its distinction between investigatory and adjudicative information in *Detroit Free Press*?

3. *Media Access to Terrorism Trials.* In the ongoing criminal prosecution of Zacarias Moussaoui for his alleged involvement in the September 11 terrorist attacks (see p. 92 in this Supplement), a consortium of media companies asserted common law and First Amendment rights of access to sealed records of pleadings, discovery materials, and oral

Chapter 15. Public Access to National Security Information 147

arguments that included some information classified top secret. The court rejected the government's argument that the Classified Information Procedures Act (CIPA), 18 U.S.C. App. 3 §§1-16 (2000) (described at casebook pp. 880-888), could alone override a constitutional right of access. United States v. Moussaoui, No. 03-4162, 2003 WL 21076836 (4th Cir. May 13, 2003), at *3. Instead, the court determined that the "interest of the public in the flow of information is protected by our exercising independent judgment concerning redactions" of materials from the records. *Id.* at *4. As for access to appellate proceedings, the court ordered bifurcated hearings. Arguments not involving the discussion of classified information would be open to the public, while others would be conducted in a sealed courtroom, followed by the prompt release of a redacted transcript. *Id.* at *6.

F. PROTECTING "STATE SECRETS" IN CIVIL LITIGATION

Page 977. Add this material to Note 5.

The Supreme Court's landmark 1953 decision in United States v. Reynolds grew out of the crash in 1948 of a B-29 bomber. Surviving family members of three civilian engineers who perished brought suit for damages under the Federal Tort Claims Act. When they sought access through discovery to the official accident report, the Supreme Court accepted without question the Air Force's assertion that disclosure of the report would "seriously hamper[] national security." The Court refused even to order in camera review of the report. When the report was declassified many years later, it was found to contain nothing whatever that could have been helpful to the nation's enemies, but instead to show pilot error, a failure to carry out special safety orders, and a history of maintenance problems with the B-29. In early 2003, surviving *Reynolds* plaintiffs and their heirs filed a petition for a writ of error *coram nobis* in the Supreme Court, asking it to set aside its half-century-old ruling on grounds that the Court was defrauded by government misrepresentation of the contents of the report. *See http://www.fas.org/sgp/jud/reynoldspet.pdf. See also* Timothy Lynch, *An Injustice Wrapped In a Pretense,* Wash. Post, June 22, 2003, at B3. However, their petition was denied without comment on June 23, 2003. In re Herring, 123 S. Ct. 2633 (2003) (Mem.). Can you guess why the Court refused to reopen the case? What does this development suggest about the role of courts in considering state secrets privilege claims?

Chapter 15. Public Access to National Security Information

Page 979. Add this material at the end of Note 9.

When the decision in Doe v. Tenet, 99 F. Supp. 2d 1284 (W.D. Wash. 2000), was appealed, the Ninth Circuit permitted the claim against the CIA for compensation for espionage services to go forward. 329 F.3d 1135 (9th Cir. 2003). "[B]ecause the net result of refusing to adjudicate the Does' claims is to sacrifice their asserted constitutional interests to the security of the nation as a whole," said the court, "both the government and the courts need to consider discretely, rather than by formula, whether this is a case in which there is simply no acceptable alternative to that sacrifice." *Id.* at 1146. "*Totten* permits dismissal of cases in which it is asserted that the very subject matter is a state secret only *after* complying with the formalities and court investigation requirements that have developed since *Totten* within the framework of the state secrets doctrine." *Id.* at 1149. Thus, the government was required to formally assert its state secrets privilege, leaving the court to test that assertion by conducting in camera and ex parte review of documents. The court also said it would make "every effort" to find ways to adjudicate the plaintiffs' claims while protecting the national security, including in camera proceedings, sealing or redaction of records, requiring security clearances for court personnel and attorneys, protective orders, and a bench trial. *Id.* at 1148-1149, 1153. By contrast, the court in Trulock v. Lee, Nos. 02-1476, 02-1477 2003 WL 21267827 (4th Cir. June 3, 2003), dismissed a suit on grounds that "state secrets are critical to the resolution of core factual issues in the case," based solely on government affidavits describing the nature of privileged information. *Id.* at *3. *See also* McDonnell Douglas Corp. v. United States, 323 F.3d 1006 (Fed. Cir. 2003).